Wiktoria Dorosz

Subjective Vision and Human Relationships in the Novels of Rosamond Lehmann

UPPSALA 1975

Doctoral dissertation at Uppsala university 1975.

© Wiktoria Dorosz

Phototypesetting:
TEXTGRUPPEN I UPPSALA AB
Printed in Sweden 1975
Liber-Tryck, Stockholm ISBN 91-554-0304-2

Table of Contents

Acknowledgements

I should like to thank Professor Gunnar Sorelius for his most kind and generous assistance, Dr. Ishrat Lindblad, who supervised the dissertation, for her help and advice, and Dr. Birgit Bramsbäck for her useful critical comments. I should also like to express my gratitude to Dr. Sven-Johan Spånberg for his words of encouragement at a stage when it was most needed, to Mr David Minugh for his perspicacious criticism, to Mr David Evans for the stylistic improvements, and to Mr Hermann Wüscher for valuable editorial suggestions.

Introduction

The present dissertation is concerned with the six novels of Rosamond Lehmann: *Dusty Answer* (1927), *A Note in Music* (1930), *Invitation to the Waltz* (1932), *The Weather in the Streets* (1936), *The Ballad and the Source* (1944), and *The Echoing Grove* (1953). Besides these novels Rosamond Lehmann has written one play, *No More Music* (1939), and a collection of short stories, *The Gypsy's Baby* (1946), which, however, are not examined here. This is because I am primarily interested in the novel as a genre, and different laws would prevail for a discussion of similar subjects in other genres. My chief concern in this thesis is with the various aspects of the subjective vision of life, as it manifests itself both on the level of form and content in the novels.

Rosamond Lehmann's first novel, *Dusty Answer,* was a bestseller on publication. The poet and editor John Lehmann, the novelist's brother, describes how the book brought her

fans and fan-mail, in which letters of perceptive, heart-warming praise from shrewd critics were mixed up with bedlamite outpourings of hysteria, reckless intimate confidences from unknown pilgrims of eternity of both sexes, proposals of marriage from the Colonies, unsolicited illegible manuscripts from aspiring authors who saw her as soul-mate and star disclosed by Heaven to guide them, demands for immediate cash support and love-sonnets from remote Alpine monasteries.[1]

The success of *Dusty Answer* remained unsurpassed by Rosamond Lehmann's subsequent novels, for in the years 1927–1952 the novel appeared in eleven more editions.[2] All her novels, however, found immediate favour with the reading public and have been translated into French, German, Spanish, Swedish, Danish, Rumanian, Italian, Finnish, Polish, Norwegian, Czech, and Dutch.[3] The novels were also widely reviewed (see bibliography, p. 137–38) and the critics were often enthusiastic. According to

[1] J. Lehmann, *The Whispering Gallery: Autobiography I* (London: Longmans, 1955), p. 134.
[2] *Dusty Answer.* London: Chatto, 1927; New York: Holt, 1927; London: Chatto 1928; New York: Grosset, 1928 (Novels of Distinction); London: Chatto, 1930 (Phoenix Library); New York: Grosset, 1930; London: Chatto, 1933 (Centaur Library); London: Penguin, 1936; London: Chatto, 1947; London: Albatros, 1947 (Albatros Modern Continental Library); New York: Reynal and Hitchock, [1947]; London: Heinemann, 1952 (Vanguard Library, 12).
[3] See Margaret T. Gustafson, "Rosamond Lehmann: A Bibliography", in *Twentieth Century Literature: A Scholarly and Critical Journal.* Vol. IV, 58–59.

Joseph Warren Beach, for example, *Dusty Answer* was "a triumphant instance of the vogue of the limited point of view",[4] George Dangerfield maintained that some of her "portraits of children and adolescents . . . are almost unequalled in our time",[5] R. A. Scott-James thought that there was no "living English novelist whose work, at its best, and within its limits, so nearly reaches artistic perfection as Rosamond Lehmann's".[6]

Despite this popularity and critical praise Rosmond Lehmann's reputation has definitely declined in the last two decades. It is certainly symptomatic of this situation that David Daiches decided to leave out his reference to Rosamond Lehmann from the 1960 edition of *The Novel and the Modern World*. One of the reasons may be that Rosamond Lehmann has been silent as a novelist since 1953 and critics no longer can view her as a promising writer of whom it was even said—after the first three novels—that "in one sense, Miss Lehmann has accomplished more than her contemporaries and has as great a promise as any of them"[7] and that she "could take a major place in modern British fiction".[8] Even though her appeal to the reading public has evidently also decreased, and the novels lost some of the attraction that a depiction of a contemporary scene usually confers on fiction, is is my conviction that they remain worth reading and interesting if only because they exemplify some significant trends present in much modern literature. I use the word "modern" as defined by Leon Edel: a novel is modern "in that it reflects the deeper and more searching *inwardness* of our century".[9] This inwardness is in turn closely related to what I call the "subjective vision of the world", which is the central concept throughout my discussion of the novels.

So far there has appeared only one critical book devoted entirely to Rosamond Lehmann: it is Diana LeStourgeon's *Rosamond Lehmann,* published in 1965.[10] This study gives an account of the novelist's family background and then, in chronological order, discusses each of her novels according to their "dominant qualities":[11] *A Note in Music,* for example, is analysed mainly in terms of its imagery, *The Echoing Grove*—of structure, *The Ballad and the Source* as a study of character. Diana LeStourgeon examines the main themes, gives an evaluation of the novels (there is also a

---

[4] J. W. Beach, *The Twentieth Century Novel* (New York: Appleton, 1932), p. 280.
[5] G. Dangerfield, "Rosamond Lehmann and the perilous enchantment of things past", *The Bookman,* LXXVI (February, 1933), 178.
[6] R. A. Scott-James, *Fifty Years of English Literature* (London: Longmans, 1951), p. 180.
[7] Dangerfield, p. 172.
[8] Ibid.
[9] L. Edel, *The Psychological Novel 1900—1950* (New York: J. B. Lippincott Co., 1955), p. 40.
[10] New York: Twayne, 1965.
[11] LeStourgeon, preface, p. 8.

10

brief chapter devoted to the short stories), and sums up Rosamond Lehmann's contribution to English literature:

equipped with an understanding of family life and of social classes and gifted with a beautiful prose style and an extraordinary insight into the thought processes of children and women, she has created out of her vision six novels, every one of which attests to the mark of the superior craftsman, and two of which lie close to that faint line which separates the near-great from the great novel. If she is not a Bach of the novel, she most assuredly is a Chopin.[12]

The scope of experience presented in the novels is perhaps restricted, but Rosamond Lehmann is aware of her limitations and stays within her range. One might define her fiction as a subjective exploration into the true nature of experience, in which there emerges no complete vision of life but rather a convincing picture of how life is felt by a handful of characters. Therein lies her claim to distinction, as well as in the organic unity of the form and themes of her novels. One of the aims of the present dissertation will be to reveal how she achieves this unity, and in order to examine this more closely, I shall first analyse the formal organization of the novels, and then describe the few main recurrent themes. Both these procedures will attempt to indicate the organizing principle of form and content: the subjective vision of life.

I am well aware of the fact that, as A. A. Mendilow puts it, "to deal with the various aspects of fiction which coexist simultaneously is to draw lines in water",[13] and yet for any analytical purposes it seems to be the only possible way. I have divided my material into four chapters, of which the first has the character of an introduction, where I propose to put Rosamond Lehmann in a certain characteristic, "metahistorical" perspective by treating her as a representative of a particular category of writers which will be defined as the *yin* group. The following two chapters are primarily concerned with an examination of the subjective vision of life as it is established on the plane of the narrative technique and characterization, whereas the fourth chapter sets out to demonstrate the importance of this subjective vision for the presentation of human relationships in the novels. Each of the three main chapters (II, III and IV) is preceded by a short introduction explaining the aims and concerns of the respective sections.

As a rule the novels will be examined separately within each section, for I believe that one should not lose sight of the fact that each of them is a separate entity; we would not, I think, be justified in treating, for example, the particular point of view of a given novel otherwise than individually. Whenever the nature of the subject seems to permit it, however, I move from one novel to another more freely, in order to relieve the monotony of a "one by one" survey. This occurs, for example, in Chapter II, Section 3, devoted

[12] Ibid., p. 144.
[13] A. A. Mendilow, *Time and the Novel* (New York: Humanities Press, 1972), p. 235.

to the handling of distance and immediacy in the presentation of the characters' experience.

Although an extrinsic approach can undoubtedly throw some light on literature, my assumption is that, in the words of R. Wellek and A. Warren, "the study of literature should, first and foremost, concentrate on the actual works of art themselves."[14] It does not seem to me that introducing biographical material could be of much help in the discussion of a writer's literary achievement. Moreover, this has already been dealt with by Diana LeStourgeon in some detail.[15] Ideally a combination of both intrinsic and extrinsic approaches to literature has perhaps most to offer, but since such an exhaustive study would be beyond the scope of the present dissertation, my intention is to confine the discussion to the novels themselves. As far as the more general background of the literary history of the period is concerned, I have included only as much of it as directly pertains to my descriptive analysis of the novels. Therefore it is found mainly in Chapter IV, Section 3, dealing with the fragmentation of life. There exist a large number of comprehensive and illuminating studies which I have found helpful and which can be recommended in this context.[16]

It is perhaps still too early to assess Rosamond Lehmann's place in modern English fiction, although such an attempt would certainly be of interest, since critics differ widely in their evaluation of her achievement. John McCormick detected in her fiction—more specifically, in *The Echoing Grove*—"the ambitiousness essential to greatness, a mastery of structure, an absolute command of prose diction, an awareness of both the lineal and spatial possibilities of fiction, a consciousness of history and politics"[17]—while Honor Tracy felt that "it would be possible to make short work of this long

---

[14] René Wellek and Austin Warren, *Theory of Literature* (Harmondsworth: Penguin, 1963), p. 139.

[15] LeStourgeon, pp. 15—28.

[16] Quentin Bell, *Virgina Woolf: A Biography* (London: The Hogarth Press, 1972), Anthony Burgess, *The Novel Now* (London: Faber & Faber, 1971), Frederick C. Crews, *E. M. Forster: The Perils of Humanism* (Princeton: Princeton Univ. Press, 1962), David Daiches, *The Novel and the Modern World* (Chicago: Chicago Univ. Press, 1948), Leon Edel, *The Psychological Novel* (New York: J. B. Lippincott Co., 1955), Alan Friedman, *The Turn of the Novel* (London, Oxford, New York: Oxford Univ. Press, 1970), J. Isaacs, *An Assessment of Twentieth-Century Literature* (London: Secker & Warburg, 1951), John Lehmann, *The Whispering Gallery* (London: Longmans, 1955), *I Am My Brother* (London: Longmans, 1960), *The Ample Proposition: Autobiography III* (London: Eyre & Spottiswoode, 1966), John McCormick, *Catastrophe and Imagination* (London, New York, Toronto: Longmans, 1957), José Ortega y Gasset, *The Dehumanization of Art* (Princeton: Princeton Univ. Press, 1948), H. V. Routh, *English Literature and Ideas in the Twentieth Century* (London: Methuen, 1946), Mark Schorer, *Society and Self in the Novel* (New York: Columbia Univ. Press, 1956), Stephen Spender, *The Struggle of the Modern* (London: Methuen, 1965), Paul West, *The Modern Novel* (London: Hutchinson, 1963).

[17] McCormick, *Catastrophe and Imagination*, p. 66.

novel [i.e. *The Echoing Grove*] in homely words that the printer very likely would refuse to set up."[18] According to a recent evaluation of the same book in F. R. Karl's *Guide to the Contemporary English Novel* (1972), *The Echoing Grove* is Rosamond Lehmann's most effective novel which, however, "partially fails ... because her characters are monotonous and fail to develop."[19] The same critic's more general stricture is that "her novels do lack intensity. While she catches agony and suffering in a phrase or sentence, she is unable to integrate these qualities into the development of her characters, often they appear as sharply-conceived fragments."[20] There is some truth in this judgement, and one of my aims will be to set this particular trait of Rosamond Lehmann's novels in a broader perspective: to treat it not only as an individual characteristic, but as a symptom of a more general phenomenon (cf. Chapter IV, Section 3). Her position as a novelist in the modern world is further investigated in the conclusion. If this dissertation succeeds in presenting Rosamond Lehmann both as a unique novelist and as a representative of her age, my aim will have been realized.

[18] Honor Tracy, "New Novels", *The New Statesman and Nation,* N.S. XLV (April 11, 1953), 433.
[19] F. R. Karl, *A Reader's Guide to the Contemporary English Novel* (London: Thomas and Hudson, 1972), p. 279.
[20] Ibid.

Chapter I

Rosamond Lehmann as a *Yin* Novelist

In this chapter I shall discuss a characteristic quality of Rosamond Lehmann's novels and try to show that it represents a certain type of literature. I realize that to classify a writer within a mode or vein of writing, disregarding the more or less traceable but always complex historical influences, is no easy task. Most of our literary-historical categories tend to be vague, abstract and general unless they refer to definite schools of writing confined within a particular time (for example naturalism, surrealism, dadaism). At the same time they are susceptible to semantic change precisely in so far as they arouse discussion and enjoy wide circulation. Rosamond Lehmann, because of her preoccupation with a subjective vision of life, may be placed within a broadly conceived Romantic tradition. In Romanticism, says Edmund Wilson,

the writer is either his own hero, or unmistakably identified with his hero, and the personality and emotions of the writer are presented as the principal subject of interest. Racine, Molière, Congreve and Swift ask us to be interested in what they have made; but Chateaubriand, Musset, Byron and Wordsworth ask us to be interested in themselves. And they ask us to be interested in themselves by virtue of the intrinsic value of the individual: they vindicate the rights of the individual against the claims of society as a whole . . . [1]

Such a broad division has the advantage, or disadvantage, of being ahistorical and thus applicable to all literature. Indeed, it is quite similar to the psychological concept of introversion and extraversion which was first put forward by C. G. Jung[2] but has since entered everyday language and often become synonymous with the pair of opposites internal-external. And so to classify Rosamond Lehmann as a Romantic is to get entangled in necessarily sweeping generalizations.

A much narrower, and consequently safer, criterion is that of the dramatic vs. the panoramic novel, where the first "excludes wide areas in order to

---

[1] Edmund Wilson, *Axel's Castle* (New York: Scribner, 1955), p. 2.
[2] Frieda Fordham, *An Introduction to Jung's Psychology* (Harmondsworth: Penguin, 1964), Chapter 2.

scrutinize a narrow segment of life", and the second "embraces and orders great expanses of human experiences".[3] But this division is not much more helpful. For while it clearly emerges that Rosamond Lehmann has been exclusively concerned with the dramatic novel, the concept does not seem to touch the essence of her writing.

Better fitted to Rosamond Lehmann's air of subjectivity, her delicate "feminine" touch which can reveal all shades of a look or gesture, is the category of *yin*, suggested by a contemporary writer and critic who has made use of the traditional terms of ancient Chinese philosophy: *yin* and *yang*.[4] In his book *The Novel Now*, Anthony Burgess recognizes

two distinct, opposite and complementary, impulses in the novel, which we can designate by the Chinese terms *yin* and *yang*—the feminine and masculine poles in a ... metaphorical sense. The *yin* ... is concerned with the colour and texture of life, the *yang* with its dynamic: the *yin* prose style is careful, exquisite, full of qualified statements, while the *yang* is less scrupulous, coarser, more aggressive. Henry James was a *yin* novelist; Ernest Hemingway belonged to the brotherhood of the *yang*. In the greatest geniuses the two meet, are reconciled, fertilize each other.[5]

Grouping writers in respect of this quality seems more satisfactory than speaking about women novelists as one particular group. George Eliot or Iris Murdoch may be said to belong to the *yang* novelists, while Samuel Richardson or Marcel Proust are more typical of the *yin*. It would be, however, quite pointless to categorize all novelists according to this division, because in many these two types of writing alternate, or sometimes their distinctive character simply does not manifest itself. Nevertheless this distinction, conceived of as a tendency rather than as a clear-cut category, seems to be fruitful. Without attempting its full definition here, I want to develop it a little further and discuss Rosamond Lehmann as a representative of the *yin* type of writing.

The *yin* quality of a writer can be recognized both in the choice of subject matter and in the way of handling it. The subject matter is as a rule narrowed down to interpersonal relationships in a limited social range, with no attempt at panoramic vistas. It is an exposition of the nuances of human intercourse, of the fine discriminations which are often disregarded by the writers concerned with the wider issues of the human predicament. Those nuances are clearly visible in, for example, Rosamond Lehmann's description of Olivia's emotional uneasiness and mounting exasperation at having to dance with an elderly man in *Invitation to the Waltz*:

[3] *Dictionary of World Literary Terms*, ed. J. T. Shipley (London: Allen & Unwin, 1970), p. 219.
[4] *A Source Book in Chinese Philosophy*, trans. and compiled by Wing-Tsit Chan (Princeton: Princeton Univ. Press, 1955), pp. 244—250, et passim.
[5] Anthony Burgess, *The Novel Now*, p. 122.

"I lost my dear wife three years ago. We were everything to each other."

What was it in the way he said this that froze the springs of sympathy? Perhaps the way he dropped his voice; or a sort of glibness, as if there were a crack, an unsound place concealed ... But of course it must have been a terrible grief.

"I'm so sorry. How awful for you." (p. 23)[6]

And after a few more dances:

Her senses shrank away from him. They seemed to shout their frantic distaste into his heedless, his leathery ear. I don't like you. I don't like touching you. I hate dancing with you. I can't bear you. She gave up smiling; almost gave up answering. Her face set stiffly. in utter dejection. Next dance I'll say I'm booked and go and hide in the cloakroom. But he'll know it's an excuse. It'll hurt his feelings. He'll go away and think: I'm a lonely old man. Oh, help! help! Will no one help? (p. 239)

The girl's emotional state is conveyed perfectly and with a convincing accuracy but, as Anthony Burgess writes about another *yin* novelist, Elizabeth Bowen, "this very exquisiteness is a limitation, since it is more easily placed in the service of the outer skin of life than used to probe into the fundamentals of the human experience."[7] Yet the question posed by Rosamond Lehmann or Virginia Woolf is by no means a trifling one: it is no less than an attempt to enquire into the meaning of life (cf. below, p. 122).

Both *yin* and *yang* writers convey some truths about the human condition but they reveal different aspects of it. Consequently, there is no need to measure, for example, Jane Austen against Walter Scott, who himself clearly realized that the author of *Pride and Prejudice*

had a talent for describing the involvements and feelings and characters of ordinary life which is to me the most wonderful I ever met with. The Big Bow-wow strain I can do myself like any now going, but the exquisite touch which renders ordinary commonplace things and characters interesting from the truth of the description and the sentiment is denied to me.[8]

This fundamental difference between the two writers has often been pointed out by critics and reviewers.[9] As Anthony Burgess observes,[10] it can be easily referred to the distinction between *yin* and *yang*. In almost any two excerpts chosen at random from their books the difference is manifested. This is how Walter Scott, after a chapter of purely historical information, introduces a character:

[6] Lehmann, *Invitation to the Waltz* (London: Chatto, 1932), p. 236. All subsequent references are to this edition.

[7] Burgess, p. 122.

[8] Walter Scott, *The Journal* (New York: Harper & Brothers, 1891), Vol. I, p. 155.

[9] Cf., for example, Robert C. Gordon, *Under Which King? A Study of the Scottish Waverley Novels* (Edinburgh, London: Oliver & Boyd, 1969), p. 144; *Scott: The Critical Heritage*, ed. John O. Hayden (London: Routledge, 1970), p. 469—an unsigned review in *London Quarterly* from 1872, pp. 490—91—a discussion by R. H. Hutton from 1878; Hesketh Pearson, *Walter Scott* (London: Methuen, 1954), p. 191.

[10] Burgess, p. 122.

It was upon a delicious summer morning, before the sun had assumed its scorching power, and while the dews yet cooled and perfumed the air, that a youth, coming from the north-eastward, approached the ford of a small river, or rather a large brook, tributary to the Cher, near to the royal Castle of Plessis-Les-Tours, whose dark and multiplied battlements rose in the background over the extensive forest with which they were surrounded. These woodlands comprised a noble chase, or royal park, fenced by an enclosure, termed, in the Latin of the middle ages, *Plexitium*, which gives the name of Plessis to so many villages in France. The castle and village of which we particularly speak, was called Plessis-Les-Tours, to distinguish it from others, and was built about two miles to the southward of the fair town of that name, the capital of ancient Touraine, whose rich plain has been termed the Garden of France.[11]

Jane Austen's way of introducing her characters is totally dissimilar:

It is a truth universally acknowledged, that a single man in possession of a good fortune must be in want of a wife.

However little known the feelings or views of such a man may be on his first entering a neighbourhood, this truth is so well fixed in the minds of the surrounding families, that he is considered as the rightful property of some one or other of their daughters.

"My dear Mr. Bennet," said his lady to him one day, "have you heard that Netherfield Park is let at last?"

Mr. Bennet replied that he had not.

"But it is," returned she; "for Mrs. Long has just been here, and she told me all about it."

Mr. Bennet made no answer.[12]

Scott is not in a hurry to present his Quentin Durward, but he is eager to supply us with as many facts connected with the scene of action as possible. He offers a bird's eye view of the setting, and it takes a few more pages before he leaves the panoramic perspective and gives us his hero's name. Jane Austen is evidently not interested in the physical surroundings for their own sake. After a couple of introductory general statements, which at the same time indicate the type of her interest in the characters and the subject of what is to follow, she sets the scene in motion and lets the characters speak for themselves. Walter Scott's and Jane Austen's approaches are both equally valid. Therefore it seems that ultimately the *yin* and *yang* are two contrasting qualities of human sensibility. What is of consequence here, however, is not their mode of existence in the novelist's mind but the *yin* character of a work itself.

The novels of Rosamond Lehmann are, in my opinion, a perfect example of the *yin* way of writing. By introducing, however tentatively, this concept into the consideration of her work, we shall be able to perceive better the specific character of her achievement within its range. A brief comparison of

[11]Walter Scott, *Quentin Durward* (New York: Airmont Publishing Co., 1967), p. 50.

[12] Jane Austen, *Pride and Prejudice* (London: R. Bentley & Son, 1891), p. 1.

some of her novels with the work of a few major authors of different periods, who may also be described as *yin* novelists, will serve to demonstrate how this mode of writing qualifies a work's scope and techniques. Thus Rosamond Lehmann's novels will be set in "the *yin* tradition", together with Jane Austen, Henry James, and Virginia Woolf.

Literary critics very often find Jane Austen's influence in the women writers of our age.[13] It is possible, however, to maintain that there exist certain similarities between Jane Austen and Rosamond Lehmann which are due to the shared *yin* character of their work rather than to any direct influence. If we assume that the *yin* type of writing is almost exclusively concerned with a small intimately known world where the emotional and moral problems of individuals are of paramount importance, then both Jane Austen and Rosamond Lehmann are *yin* novelists. In their case the kinship manifests itself more on the side of subject matter than technique; it is obvious that the novel form evolved considerably during the century and a quarter that elapsed between the novels chosen for discussion here: *Sense and Sensibility* (1811) and *Invitation to the Waltz* (1932) and its sequel, *The Weather in the Streets* (1936).

A recurrent theme in both Jane Austen and Rosamond Lehmann is the transitional phase in women's life from girlhood to womanhood. In both writers the transition is marked by a confrontation of a sensitive individual with the codes of social behaviour. The conflict is apparently the same but it is resolved differently: even if the norms of propriety are similarly fettering to Jane Austen's Marianne Dashwood and Rosamond Lehmann's Olivia Curtis, the meaning of their social experience is not the same. Jane Austen's world is pervaded by the harmonious spirit of classicism, a sense of balance and sanity not to be attained in the modern age of disintegration of values when individuals have lost their sense of living in a more or less predictable and secure order.

It is perhaps characteristic of the *yin* sensibility that, although the two novelists live in different worlds, their response and sensitivity to certain aspects of life are analogous. Let us look closer at secrecy as an element of their heroines' worlds.

In *Sense and Sensibility* Marianne repeatedly breaks social convention and Elinor tries to screen her and cover up her eccentric conduct before society's censorious eye. The necessity of concealment is a powerful factor in the world of the novel; in fact everything pertaining to love has to be kept secret: the happy phase of Marianne's love for Willoughby, Colonel Brandon's love for Marianne, Elinor's for Edward, Lucy's engagement and marriage. It often looks like a social game which enlivens the boredom of drawing-room gatherings, but for the most part it functions as a smoke

---

[13] See Ralph Freedman, *The Lyrical Novel* (Princeton: Princeton Univ. Press, 1963), p. 227.

screen against society's restrictiveness. As Tony Tanner writes in his introduction to the book, "if secrecy is often a painful obligation imposed by the forms of a rigid society, it may also be a strategy against or around them."[14]

Secrecy still has the same function in *The Weather in the Streets,* where Olivia's relationship with Rollo Spencer is vitiated by this necessity:

no one must find out. It dashed me a bit sometimes at first, Rollo being so cautious, always in a stew for fear he'd be seen, recognized; always saying safer not, better not, better not go here, do this or that; not ring up too often at the office. . . . Quite soon I got infected with it.[15]

In *Sense and Sensibility* secrecy accompanied premarital attachments and property matters and, as the characters sooner or later complied with the social patterns, the need for concealment ceased. In *The Weather in the Streets* secrecy is directed against the fundamental social institution— marriage —and in the end society triumphs: Olivia cannot resist its pressure, personified in Lady Spencer, and agrees to give up her lover.

There is more than one similarity between Jane Austen's and Rosamond Lehmann's treatment of the social life of the middle and upper-middle classes to which they both confine themselves. The *yin* writers, with their perspicacious insights and a quick eye for absurd details, are particularly good at satirizing it. Understatement, irony, and cool detachment exhibit successfully people's inadequacies in a social context. Jane Austen writes about Lady Middleton and Mrs. John Dashwood in the following manner:

There was a kind of cold hearted selfishness on both sides, which mutually attracted them; and they sympathized with each other in an insipid propriety of demeanour, and a general want of understanding.[16]

In *The Weather in the Streets,* at a dinner-party at the house of Lady Spencer, Olivia watches her neighbour at the table:

In what career he doubtless distinguished himself—lisp, monocle and all? The aura of authority was around him; drawing rooms of taste, cultured evening parties seemed his obvious setting; upper-class Egerias his natural companions: all gracefully, spaciously, securely à la recherche du temps perdu. Connoisseur of . . . collector of . . . He suggested that sort of thing.

The savoury was before him now, rich, succulent. He was respecting it with silent gravity and concentration. (pp. 83—84)

In each of the two novels there is a pair of sisters whose characterization is executed by means of light *yin* touches: the little mannerisms of speech,

[14] Tony Tanner, introduction to *Sense and Sensibility* (Harmondsworth: Penguin, 1971), p. 12.
[15] Lehmann, *The Weather in the Streets* (London: Collins, 1951), pp. 159—60. All subsequent references are to this edition.
[16] *Sense and Sensibility*, p. 236.

19

different pastimes, tastes in clothes or ways of looking at nature of Marianne and Elinor, or Olivia and Kate, indicate a fundamental difference of temperament. We see Kate spend her evening sewing the dress for the ball, while Olivia is crying over a book read for the fifth time (see p. 98). In a similar way Jane Austen presents psychological differences in dramatic terms.[17] We can take as an example the scene where Elinor is at last free to tell Marianne about her secret suffering caused by Lucy Steele's revelation of Edward's engagement, making both Marianne and the reader realize how different and superior Elinor's conduct was when compared to Marianne's self-centred anguish.

The resemblance between Jane Austen and Rosamond Lehmann consists chiefly in a self-imposed limitation of the field of exploration and a great competence within it. Both novelists confine themselves to the world they know from first-hand experience; as a rule they do not attempt to portray male characters by entering their minds.[18] In *The Weather in the Streets* all the men are shown only as they appear to Olivia. The same holds true of Jane Austen: Willoughby, Colonel Brandon, Edward Ferras and all the others are depicted only as they reveal themselves in action, or as the women in the book (especially Elinor) imagine them, never from the inside. As a critic says, it is "a woman's world, and in it the male characters are simply symbols of the different fates in store for women."[19]

Despite the similarities, there exists a fundamental difference between the two writers in the status accorded to the experience presented in their novels. It is finally, as Erich Auerbach observed, "a matter of the author's attitude toward the reality of the world he represents. And this attitude differs entirely from that of authors who interpret the actions, situations, and characters of their personages with objective assurance, as was the general practice in earlier times."[20] Rosamond Lehmann belongs to a generation for which such assurance was no longer possible. It is also evident that, although Rosamond Lehmann's novels share some *yin* traits with Jane Austen's writing, they produce an altogether different effect because their organization and style are very remote from the composed tone of the older writer. This has been caused, to a large extent, by a new mode of narration in Rosamond Lehmann which would have been hardly possible without the achievement of Henry James. Rosamond Lehmann employs in all her novels a subjective narrative technique, that is, she presents her material filtered through the consciousness of one or more characters. Henry James is the generally acknowledged father of this device of the limited point of view, which is

---

[17] Cf. below, p. 72.

[18] Rosamond Lehmann's not altogether successful exception is the character of Rickie Masters in *The Echoing Grove*.

[19] David Daiches, *A Study of Literature* (New York: Cornell Univ. Press, 1948), p. 115.

[20] Erich Auerbach, *Mimesis* (Princeton: Princeton Univ. Press, 1971), p. 535.

20

extremely appropriate to the specific concerns of the *yin* writers (though by no means exclusive to them) for it enables them to probe deeper into the world of thoughts and emotions. In the two novels discussed below—Henry James's *What Maisie Knew* (1897) and Rosamond Lehmann's *The Ballad and the Source*—the interest lies in the growing awareness of a child. Both novelists explore their heroines' psychology by means of the Jamesian method which enhances the *yin* quality of these novels. Therefore it may be helpful to describe more closely the Jamesian method which, together with the subjectivism of the modern novel, makes both for amplification and for sophistication of the *yin* tendency.

Henry James was well aware of the significance of his consciously elaborated way of telling a story which he described as

my preference for dealing with my subject-matter, for "seeing my story," through the opportunity and the sensibility of some more or less detached, some not strictly involved, though thoroughly interested and intelligent, witness or reporter, some person who contributes to the case mainly a certain amount of criticism and interpretation of it. . . . the terms of this person's access to [the story] and estimate of it contributing thus by some fine little law to intensification of interest.[21]

Henry James's preoccupation with the questions of form increased with the years and, particularly in his later novels, produced effects verging on obscurity. I shall therefore discuss here *What Maisie Knew*, which is a "moderate" example of James's manner but in which all the basic principles of his "preference" are present.

A similarity of both theme and method in *The Ballad and the Source* to *What Maisie Knew* has been noted by Diana Trilling in her review of Rosamond Lehmann's book:

[It] is a psychological mystery of the type that Henry James delighted in, and from the precocious children who see and hear such a large part of the story, through the careful architecture of the narrative and its emphasis on psychological motive, to its atmosphere of well-bred horror *The Ballad and the Source* reveals its distinguished ancestry. Even the names of the characters suggest the connection.[22]

In James's novel Maisie's unfortunate family background failed to condition her as to what she is to expect from people: she takes for granted the fact that her mother does not care for her because it has never been otherwise in her short life. Therefore she does not condemn Ida but suffers her humours as if such were the nature of things and she is able to experience much wickedness without bitterness. In short, James's choice of a child as the "witness" offered him an original perspective on morals and manners.

---

[21] Henry James, *The Art of the Novel: Critical Prefaces*, ed. R. P. Blackmur (New York: Scribner, 1935), p. 327.
[22] Diana Trilling, "Fiction in Review", *The Nation*, CLX (April 14, 1945), 423.

Rosamond Lehmann makes similar use of her young heroine Rebecca in *The Ballad and the Source*. The novel resembles *What Maisie Knew* in that it also presents a complex story as it reveals itself to a curious and sensitive young girl. Mrs. Jardine, a woman with a past, befriends her beloved old friend's granddaughter Rebecca. Mrs. Jardine is a very unconventional old lady whose principle is to treat the young without condescension and to tell them, according to her own claims, only the truth. She particularly attracts the romantic and impressionable child Rebecca by her sophisticated poetical way of expressing herself, by her elegance and kindness. Rebecca is also flattered by Mrs. Jardine's choice of her, so young, as a confidante. The interplay between these two characters serves to disclose them to the reader in a subtle and convincing way.

The development of both Rebecca and Maisie is shown through their changing attitudes: Maisie's conception of Sir Claude's nature, as well as Rebecca's growing awareness of the complexities of Mrs. Jardine's behaviour, is modified with the passage of time. These changes are captured and described in the very moment they take place, as when Maisie is growing suspicious of Sir Claude's integrity for the first time:

There came to her from this glance at what they might hide the first small glimpses of something in him that she would n't have expected. There had been times when she had had to make the best of the impression that she was herself deceitful; yet she had never concealed anything bigger than a thought. Of course she now concealed this thought of how strange it would be to see *him* hide; and while she was so actively engaged he continued: "Besides, you know, I'm not afraid of your father."[23]

A similar realization comes to Rebecca in a conversation with Mrs. Jardine:

Once more in this caressing garden [. . .] intimations of desolation brushed me, made me shiver. The worm was under the leaf. "Cunning" echoed in the same land as "ruin," "treachery," "fall."
Mrs. Jardine, pausing at the end of the herbaceous border, mused. For the first time in her actual presence the sense pierced me directly: that she was wicked. But when next moment I looked up at her, there was her profile lifted beautifully above me, serene and reassuring as a symbol in stone.[24]

The style of the two passages is different, but the sureness and delicacy of touch in their careful examination of the workings of child psychology and their penetrating portrayal of the gradual changes in the girl's judgement and insight are remarkable in both novelists. These qualities are characteristic of the *yin* type of writing which registers even the smallest and hardly discernible movements of consciousness. This is not to say that they are exclusively *yin* qualities; undoubtedly many of the traits described here as *yin*

[23] Henry James, *What Maisie Knew* (London: Oxford Univ. Press, 1966), p. 69.
[24] Lehmann, *The Ballad and the Source* (London: Collins, 1944), p. 104. All subsequent references are to this edition.

are characteristic of much modern post-Jamesian fiction. Nonetheless they are particularly in keeping with the *yin* concerns as described above.

James's interest in the way the human mind works, in motivation and slight, outwardly insignificant events taking place in the characters' awareness, has grown into almost an obsession in the novels of Rosamond Lehmann's older contemporary, Virginia Woolf. In her fiction, *Mrs. Dalloway* (1922) marks the transference of the scene of action to the characters' minds, at the expense of external plot, which becomes reduced to a minimum. This method has its perils for the novel form: in the exploration of the subtle movements of individual consciousness—expressed through impressions, wandering associations and sensations—characters lose their continuity and tend to disappear as well-defined personalities in a story. Virginia Woolf reveals consciousness in its contingency and lack of logic by means of the stream of consciousness method. Rosamond Lehmann does not go so far on the way of changing the novel into a medium for poetry.[25] Unlike Virginia Woolf, she maintains a balance between the subjective and objective aspects of her characters. She presents individual consciousness in its interpersonal relations.

Virginia Woolf's fiction forms a conscious and elaborate application of her theoretical notions about what a modern novel should be. Her views on the subject of "the proper stuff of fiction" are expressed in her famous essay "Modern Fiction" (1919). Her criticism of Wells, Bennett, Galsworthy—"the materialists" as she calls them (we may say here "the *yang* writers")—is that "they write of unimportant things . . . they spend immense skill and immense industry making the trivial and transitory appear the true and enduring."[26] They are disappointing because they do not tell us about life, only about insignificant details accumulated to produce an impression of life. She wrote: "an ordinary mind on an ordinary day receives a myriad impressions",[27] which constitute our experience but are dismissed by the materialists. The task of the novelist is to convey precisely what they ignore: this "luminous halo" in which our consciousness is enwrapped, instead of building a conventional plot.

In another famous and often quoted essay entitled "Mr. Bennett and Mrs. Brown" (1924), Virginia Woolf asserts that in our century a tremendous event has taken place: human character has changed. And as the study of character is the novelist's primary interest, he must find new means for describing it, for the tools of one generation are useless for the next.[28]

---

[25] Cf. Malcolm Bradbury, *Possibilities: Essays on the State of the Novel* (London, Oxford, New York: Oxford Univ. Press, 1973), p. 6.

[26] Virginia Woolf, "Modern Fiction", *The Common Reader* (London: The Hogarth Press, 1948), p. 187.

[27] Ibid., p. 189.

[28] See Viriginia Woolf, "Mr. Bennett and Mrs. Brown", *The Captain's Death Bed* (London: The Hogarth Press, 1950), pp. 103–104.

Virginia Woolf's novels are such experiments and so, on a smaller scale, are the novels of Rosamond Lehmann: both writers sought new, adequate ways of expressing the new conception of character. Rosamond Lehmann may be said to have gone only part of the innovative way that Virginia Woolf took. Yet the *yin* traits of all their works permit us to group them together perhaps more confidently than their common awareness of the new situation of art in the modern world, which they share with writers as different from them (and each other) as D. H. Lawrence and Joseph Conrad.

A correspondence of method between Virginia Woolf and Rosamond Lehmann is visible, for example, in *Night and Day* (1919) and *A Note in Music* (1930). *Night and Day* is a traditional novel among Virginia Woolf's works, with a story *sensu stricto,* involving love complications happily resolved at the end. The happy ending brought about by the comical Mrs. Hillbury and the social comedy that the novel contains (Mr. Clacton, Mrs. Seale) are in the broad tradition of the English novel. But this early book already reveals Virginia Woolf's inclinations: external events are less important than the inner world of Katharine Hillbury, Mary Datchet, and Ralph Denham. The representation of various minds and their perception of being alive and being in love forms the centre of *Night and Day*, as well as of *A Note in Music*. In both novels description is subjected to this end: Virginia Woolf and Rosamond Lehmann describe how a place feels like rather than what it looks like. For example, the description of the moors in *A Note in Music,* as seen by Grace Fairfax, intimates simultaneously what they meant to her:

In the west a mass of darker clouds marked the defeat of the battered and struggling day. It was sad on the moors, and the wind blew with a chill whistle. The wild birds cried and flew. There was a gull from the sea, flying high up, with the wind, on motionless wings. At the top of the slope she looked far out over shadowy dramatic wastes of land, and saw the sea, laid in a dark line along the horizon.[29]

Grace's mood is reinforced by the atmosphere of the moors and *vice versa,* her perception of them is affected by her mood. Some descriptions in *Night and Day* have a similar function:

the stars did their usual work upon the mind, froze to cinders the whole of our short human history, and reduced the human body to an ape-like, furry form, crouching amid the brushwood of a barbarous clod of mud. This stage was soon succeeded by another, in which there was nothing in the universe save stars and the light of stars; as she looked up the pupils of her eyes so dilated with starlight that the whole of her seemed dissolved in silver and spilt over the ledges of the stars for ever and ever indefinitely through space.[30]

---

[29] Lehmann, *A Note in Music* (London: Chatto, 1930), p. 37. All subsequent references are to this edition.

[30] Virginia Woolf, *Night and Day* (London: The Hogarth Press, 1960), p. 533.

Obviously the device of the pathetic fallacy has always been used by a great many writers, but it acquires a particular prominence in the novelists whose characters—like many characters of Virginia Woolf and practically all Rosamond Lehmann heroines—depend to a high degree on feeling and intuition as the significant ways of relating to people and things.

The dramatic episodes in both novels are interwoven with the lyrical passages in the form of interior monologues. They are more numerous in *A Note in Music* than in *Night and Day*, but the later novels of Virginia Woolf may be said to consist entirely of them. These monologues are often written not in the stream of consciousness technique but reported by the undramatized narrator,[31] who provides both an inside and an outside perspective on the characters.

In *Night and Day* the shift from one character to another is governed by the exigencies of the plot to such an extent that, when a partner is needed for William Rodney, Cassandra is introduced after the first three fourths of the novel. But already in Virginia Woolf's next novel, *Jacob's Room*, the plot is sacrificed to the search for truth about Jacob: the only link between characters is that they belong, however marginally, to Jacob's world.

In *Night and Day* as well as in *A Note in Music*, the small group of central characters offers a social panorama—the often uneasy class feelings and prejudices are acutely hinted at. The social aspects of people are contrasted with their often contradictory inner selves: Katharine is quite different from the person that her circle takes her for; similarly Grace, a most withdrawn and seemingly apathetic woman, is in fact a poet of great sensitivity and inner intensity. A collection of several persons of different social standing produces an impression of "density" and "breadth" of life, though the primary interest lies in their dimension in "depth".

A Note in Music seems to lie half way between *Night and Day* and *Mrs. Dalloway* as far as the proportion between presentation of mental states and outward action is concerned. The passages describing subjective experiences deal with the fundamental questions in the lives of the characters and they give meaning to the often insignificant events of the plot. Virginia Woolf analyses usually trivial occurrences in their disproportionate effect on the mind; they release chains of thoughts and moods which are reported faithfully and painstakingly. Mrs. Dalloway's morning walk is not important as an element in the story: it has a meaning in itself, because it captures her experience of being alive. In Virginia Woolf's attempt to give the fullest impression of existence the books sometimes tend to become diffuse: she concentrates on sensation at the expense of action. Rosamond Lehmann's novels are always carefully constructed and there are no "loose ends" in

---

[31] For the distinction between dramatized and undramatized narrators see Wayne Booth, *The Rhetoric of Fiction* (Chicago: Chicago Univ. Press, 1961), p. 151.

them. All the episodes fall into place and are relevant to the main subject: they all contribute to the picture of a definite love relationship (*The Weather in the Streets*), a particular story (*The Ballad and the Source*), a specific experience (*Invitation to the Waltz*). Nevertheless, here again, just as in the comparisons with Jane Austen and Henry James, we can speak, despite the substantial differences, of a common quality underlying the writings of Virginia Woolf and Rosamond Lehmann. There is in both novelists the peculiar *yin* character, an intimacy of treatment where things large *and* small compose the fabric of life. Two random passages may serve to illustrate this quality:

She began to go slowly upstairs, with her hand on the banisters, as if she had left a party [. . .] had shut the door and gone out and stood alone, a single figure against the appalling night, or rather, to be accurate, against the stare of this matter-of-fact June morning; soft with the glow of petals for some, she knew, and felt it, as she paused by the open staircase window which let in blinds flapping, dogs barking, let in, she thought, feeling herself suddenly shrivelled, aged, breastless, the grinding, blowing, flowering of the day out of doors, out of the window, out of her body and brain which now failed, since Lady Bruton, whose lunch parties were said to be extraordinarily amusing, had not asked her. (*Mrs. Dalloway*, p. 35[32])

And a passage from Rosamond Lehmann:

the book taken up, the book laid down, aghast, because of the traffic's sadness, which was time, lamenting and pouring away down all the streets for ever; because of the lives passing up and down outside with steps and voices of futile purpose and forlorn commotion: draining out my life, out of the window, in their echoing wake, leaving me dry, stranded, sterile, bound solitary to the room's minute respectability, the gas-fire, the cigarette, the awaited bell, the gramophone's idiot companionship, the unyielding arm-chair, the narrow bed, the hot-water bottles I must fill, the sleep I must sleep. . . . (*The Weather in the Streets*, p. 77)

The stress on physical sensations produces the effect of concreteness, and the enumerative syntax renders the mood of monotonous sadness. The feelings of both Clarissa Dalloway and Olivia Curtis are conveyed with *yin* precision of recording, full of qualifications demanded by the novelists' concern with a faithful representation of the inner lives of their heroines.

The term *yin* has been used here to signal and indicate, rather than define, a certain quality in writing. The *yin/yang* opposition, as we have seen, cuts across some well established critical categories according to which the romanticism of both Walter Scott and Rosamond Lehmann could be set over against the classicism of Jane Austen. Yet even these categories, as Edmund Wilson rightly cautions us, are not to be taken too rigorously:

What really happens, of course, is that one set of methods and ideas is not

---

[32] Virginia Woolf, *Mrs. Dalloway* (Harmondsworth: Penguin, 1972), p. 35.

completely superseded by another; but that, on the contrary, it thrives in its teeth—so that, on the one hand, Flaubert's prose has learned to hear, see and feel with the delicate senses of Romanticism at the same time that Flaubert is disciplining and criticizing the Romantic temperament . . . [33]

I hope that the foregoing discussion has sufficiently indicated Rosamond Lehmann's place within a qualitative "metahistorical tradition". However appropriate, *yin* is a general category and, as such, cannot become the critical tool with which to examine the essential features of an individual writer. Therefore I shall be henceforward exclusively concerned with a more distinctive, unifying characteristic of Rosamond Lehmann's writing which manifests itself in her novels as a subjective vision of life.

[33] *Axel's Castle*, pp. 10—11.

Chapter II

Subjective Vision

In the novels of Rosamond Lehmann the thoughts and emotions of the main character or characters are of central importance. The particular manner in which they are represented makes for what here will be called the subjective vision of life.

The subject of Section 1 is the limited point of view. It is the narrative method instrumental in the creation of the subjective vision of life. A particular limited point of view of a given character naturally affects—if only by determining what is to be included and what omitted—the presentation of the world in the novel. My special interest lies in the interdependence between the governing consciousness and its world, presented in what I will call "the side perspective". For the discussion of the limited point of view I use several terms as they are defined in Wayne Booth's *The Rhetoric of Fiction*.

The limited point of view determines the treatment of the time element in the novels, since individual inner time differs, by definition, from the conventional time by the clock. This typically twentieth-century concern with time manifests itself in all the six novels: Section 2 examines their time patterns which are crucial to the structure of the novel as a whole.

Section 3 is devoted to an analysis of another aspect of Rosamond Lehmann's narrative technique: the treatment of distance and immediacy. In this context are considered certain stylistic devices (such as the variations of the person in narration, *erlebte Rede,* dialogue, elliptical sentences, etc.) and their function in manipulating the distance between the reader and the represented world, as well as between various elements within this world.

1. Limited Point of View

Throughout her novels Rosamond Lehmann employs the narrative technique of the limited point of view, which is extremely appropriate to her main concern—the creation of a subjective vision of life. All her six novels can be examined as experiments in this technique, applied to an enquiry into the meaning of experience. The use of the limited point of view implies a subjective presentation of people and events. There appears no omniscient author to show us what "really" happened, but we can only see the represented world through the subjective consciousness of a person belonging in this world. There exists no "objectivity" in the sense in which it existed in Dickens's novels, for example, but only a more or less realistically restricted perspective of a central consciousness. In this section I propose to deal with the novels one after another since point of view is an aspect of the whole of a given fictional world and can only be meaningfully discussed in relation to that particular whole.

In *Dusty Answer* reality is presented through the filter of one conscious-ness. It is the story of the sensitive, lonely and romantic Judith Earle. Her childhood, adolescence, and first disappointments are influenced by a group of cousins staying next door in a country house on the Thames. Both they and all the other characters in the novel are presented as Judith experiences them: the world presented in the book is refracted through Judith's sensibility. *Dusty Answer* was praised as a novel of side perspective by David Daiches who wrote:

On *a priori* grounds it might be considered more effective to concentrate the story of a family more definitely on a central figure: this has been done with great success by Rosamond Lehmann in *Dusty Answer*, where the central figure does not belong to the family whose fortunes are followed, so that the reader has the advantage of an objective view of the family history together with the added richness provided by the interactions between a group of similar people and a single one—who is also the ob-server—dissimilar.[1]

Judith's impression of being an outsider among them is increased by what she feels to be an essential likeness among the cousins. When she meets them as an adult, she feels that

As in the old days, they formed their oppressive self-sufficient circle of blood-intimacy with its core of indifference if not hostility to the stranger. (p. 61)

And again:

she felt suddenly startled.
But they were all alike!
So strange, so diverse in feature and colour, they yet had grown up with this overpowering likeness; as if one mind had thought them all out and set upon them, in spite of variations, the unmistakable stamp of itself. (p. 88)

The use of the side perspective throws light in two directions: at the object of Judith's observation and at Judith herself as the observer-narrator. The nature of her remarks is often more revealing about her own feelings than about what she perceives, for example:

They stood around, making no effort, idly fingering and dropping the tags of conversation she offered them, as if she were the hostess and they most difficult guests. (p. 61)

or Judith's impression of Roddy:

[1] David Daiches, *The Novel and the Modern World*, p. 44.

29

with features a trifle blurred and indeterminate, as if he had just waked up; the dark hair faintly ruffled and shining, the expression secret-looking, with something proud and sensual and cynical, far older than his years. (p. 75)

Later in the evening, confused and insecure, Judith is even less able to see Roddy clearly:

At supper he sat opposite to her, and twinkled at her incessantly as if encouraging her to continue to share with him a secret joke. But, confused amongst them all, she had lost her sense of vast amusement and assurance; she was unhappy because he was a stranger laughing at her and she could not laugh back. (p. 76)

At this point Judith does not interpret Roddy for us. During the course of the same evening, however, her observation of Roddy provides a clue to his homosexual relationship with Tony, although Judith herself is not clear about it.

The narration of her thoughts and feelings (the book is written mainly in the third person) is not straightforward, since Judith is both the governing consciousness of the novel, with the function of recording events, and a participant in its action. The ensuing two aspects of her account—Judith as the narrator and Judith as one of the characters—illuminate one another:

Who could it be coming towards her down the little pathway which led from the station to the bottom of the garden and then onto the blue gate in the wall of the garden next door? She stood still under the overhanging lilacs and may-trees, her heart pounding, her limbs melting. It was Roddy, in a white shirt and white flannels—coming from the station. He caught sight of her, seemed to hesitate, came on till he was close to her; and she had the strangest feeling that he intended to pass right by her as if he did not see her. . . . What was the word for his face? Smooth: yes, smooth as a stone. She had never before noticed what a smooth face he had; but she could not see him clearly because of the beating of her pulses. (pp. 261—62)

In this passage we learn about things on different planes, as it were: first, there is the outward action—the setting of the scene, Roddy's approach, and the information about his dress. At the same time Judith the heroine gives an account of her violent emotions. Moreover, her guess at what he felt proves right, for as we learn later from their conversation, he had indeed considered passing her by without speaking at all.

Judith never tries to imagine the cousins' thoughts about other things than their feelings for each other and for herself—and these the reader can compare with their actual behaviour. Thus the subjective elements in Judith's perspective are set against the reality she witnesses. This pattern reappears in later parts of the novel and culminates in her final disenchantment, whose approach is visible to the reader at a much earlier stage, due to a double perspective on the cousins in the novel: on one level they are the romanticized creatures that Judith wants to see, and on another they are persons in their own right, shown in action in which Judith partakes. There is a paradox in Judith as a narrator: through her subjective vision an objective picture arises.

And so when Martin and Roddy unexpectedly come to visit her, Martin says:

"Julian has got some tiresome people we don't like, so we escaped, and Roddy suggested coming to find you."
Roddy raised his eyebrows, smiling faintly.
"Well, we both suggested it," continued Martin with a blush.
"May we really stay?"
Which, oh which of them suggested it? [wonders Judith]. (p. 93)

It is perfectly clear to the reader that it was Martin's idea, but because Judith would much prefer Roddy to want to see her, she allows herself to hope it was Roddy. We do not see more than Judith does but we draw different conclusions from hers. As James wrote about the perspective of his Maisie (in the Preface to *What Maisie Knew*), though it is "her relation, her activity of spirit, that determines all our concern", she has a power "of shedding a light far beyond . . . her comprehension; of lending to poorer persons and things, by the mere fact of their being involved with her and by the special scale she creates for them, a precious element of dignity."[2]

Judith is made into what Wayne Booth terms a "reliable narrator"[3] by certain qualities of character which make it possible to accept her unusual memory and power of observation. In the very first pages we read about her loneliness, sensitivity, interest in other people ("people never did remember her so hard as she remembered them", p. 4) and her yearning to understand them. Above all, we learn about her attitude towards the cousins and the special quality they assumed in her mind:

In the long spaces of being alone which they only, at rarer and rarer intervals, broke, she had turned them over, fingered them so lovingly, explored them so curiously that, melting into the darkly-shining enchanted shadow-stuff of remembered childhood, they had become well-nigh fantastic creatures. (p. 5)

Yet as far as her recollection of facts is concerned, Judith is completely trustworthy. She is capable of recalling accurately the events of her early childhood, and there appears no author as a person[4] in the novel. The fact that Judith stands alone, with no sympathetic narrator behind her (in the sense that the characters of George Eliot, for example, are not alone), makes for a decrease of emotional distance between her and the reader. Since we can see only what Judith can see, her frequently impassioned impressions and judgements set the emotional pitch of the book. They are not modified by other characters' experience, and consequently Judith's perception of the world gains in immediacy. An example can be taken from her first moments in college, where she feels abandoned and terrified. She is in Hall for the first time, just before a meal, among a crowd of noisy girls:

[2] Henry James, *What Maisie Knew*, preface, p. 7.
[3] Booth, p. 75.
[4] Cf. ibid., pp. 50—53.

There fell a silence. A voice like a bell went through the room, calling: *Benedictus benedicat.* And then came a roar—a scraping, an immense yelling that rose to the ceiling and there rolled, broke, swelled again without a pause. Beneath its volumes she felt herself lost again; but nobody appeared to have noticed it. (p. 124)

Rosamond Lehmann often presents events as remembered by Judith at the close of a day, or after many years, so that the subjective angle of vision comes in naturally, together with Judith's reflections and comments. Her memory selects only the fragments that are relevant to her present moods and emotions; for example, when she is thinking about the summer with the cousins, Roddy plays the central part in her reminiscences (pp. 100—109). This selectiveness of Judith's vision indicates the quality of her personal experience: it is clear to the reader that Roddy fascinates her more than Martin.

The single point of view has a unifying effect on the novel, however mixed its ingredients may seem. One of the first critics of *Dusty Answer,* Leonard Woolf, felt that the poetry was superimposed on the plot,[5] yet it is possible to defend it in terms of Judith's character: her poetical disposition is bound to permeate her rendering of life. Similarly the background, the setting of action, is presented exclusively through Judith's subjective perspective. There is only as much or as little of it as is relevant to Judith at a given moment, and it is highly coloured by her present mood. Examples of the pathetic fallacy abound in *Dusty Answer.* This is how her garden appears to Judith after she has arranged a rendezvous with her lover:

The sinking sun flooded the lawn. Its radiance was slit with long narrow shades [. . .] The roses were open to the very heart, fainting in their own fragrance [. . .] The weeping beech flowed downwards, a full green fountain, whispering silkily. Forms, lights, colours vibrated, burned, ached, leapt with excess of life. (p. 254)[6]

The book's ultimate success lies in the convincing creation of Judith's character achieved by means of the single point of view, which offers what J. W. Beach called "a means of steeping us imaginatively in the special and rare solution which is the essence of a unique personality."[7]

Rosamond Lehmann's second novel, *A Note in Music,* seems to be an experiment in a technique the reverse of that employed in her first book. *Dusty Answer* is a presentation of several characters (the Fyfe cousins, Judith's parents, her friend Jennifer etc.) as reflected in the "rare solution"—the sensibility of one personality; in *A Note in Music* we are concerned mainly with one character's impact on several people of very dissimilar sensibilities.

[5] Leonard Woolf, "The World of Books: Rhapsody or Dusty Answer?" *The Nation and Athenaeum,* XLI (September 10, 1927), 749.
[6] In order to avoid confusion between Rosamond Lehmann's frequently used three dots and my own ellipses the latter will be put in square brackets.
[7] Beach, p. 303.

The story is loosely centred round the disturbance an attractive young man, Hugh Miller, causes in the lives of several women in a drab provincial town. Two middle-aged wives, Grace Fairfax and Norah MacKay, and a hairdresser-prostitute Pansy come to focus their feelings, in varying degree, on Hugh, who is also the structural centre of the novel. We get to know the characters not only through their involvement with Hugh—in fact many aspects of their lives are revealed, mainly in their interior monologues—but most of the action in the book revolves round their encounters with and thoughts about him. These are all recounted by the author who remains the "undramatized narrator" (as Wayne Booth defines him), that is, the novel does not refer to him directly yet we have an implicit picture of him standing behind the scenes as stage manager.[8] He presents many different angles of vision, including that of Hugh himself, Grace's and Norah's husbands, and of various secondary figures. There is also the perspective of "collective gossip"; for instance, Norah's husband as seen by her relatives:

Gerald MacKay, penniless professor at the University, of quite different class, they said, able neither to ride nor shoot nor hold a rod; very queer too: simply an ill-mannered boor, one would say, if it were not more charitable to think that early brilliance at Cambridge, or perhaps shell-shock, had unhinged him a little, (p. 29)

or the community's view of Norah and Grace:

one had a suspicion in conversation with her [...] that she was not ... not local, not identifiable with the community in spite of her willing and capable association with the kind of activities that had their expression in bazaars and committee-meetings. She was a well-bred woman; one distinguished her indubitable County blood; her detachment was intangible and unspoken: unlike that of Mrs. Fairfax, that disagreeable woman, snobbish and exclusive without any justification whatsoever. (p. 74)

Very little information is provided directly by the author-narrator (for example, the dog's indigestion, p. 183). Some of the lyrical descriptions of nature which seem to come from the author-narrator imperceptibly glide into the consciousness of one of the characters: for instance, the February aura at the beginning of Part II:

In the southern countries February will come in with a sudden stillness, with mild blue watery air, with the ploughed earth mysterious in the dark fields, yielding to bear the young corn [...] But in the north there is no change. In February the wind-carved snow-wreaths still lie on the brown moors, old drifts heap the ditches. Should the rain unbind the earth for one day, an iron frost will lock it once again on the morrow.
There is no change at all, thought Norah, standing on Grace Farifax's doorstep and observing by means of a prolonged squint that her nose was red and besmutted. (p. 25)

Sometimes a character's perception is unusually heightened, as in the scene with Grace in the park:

[8] Cf. Booth, p. 272.

It must be the weakness of convalescence that made one so quiveringly sensitive. Forms struck one's eyes as if for the first time, sound pierced too keenly, colour and light were too living, too exquisite. The greys and browns had vanished, swept away before a torrent of blue and golden light, submerged beneath a spate of green [. . .] She heard herself cough: it was the cough of a real person. She looked down and saw herself moored to the seat as firmly as the stout old lady sitting opposite her; yet she felt the wind lift her, whirl her like a straw, a feather, in its wake. (p. 83)

Such a state of heightened awareness has been called a characteristic feature of modern literature. It consists in an "emphasis on states of abnormal impressionability with their blend of acuity and paralysis of the faculties".[9] In such a condition a chance meeting with Hugh takes on a symbolic significance for Grace. It is, however, modified for the reader by an immediate shift of perspective to Hugh, and later in the novel her misconception about his person is exposed (cf. below, pp. 97, 108—109).

The constant shifting of the narrative point of view gives an impression of fragmentariness, but out of the various fragments—different notes, as it were— a certain whole is composed. In the case of several characters of secondary importance, e.g. Christopher Seddon, the inside view does not so much reveal him to the reader as provide a centre of consciousness through which we observe a scene between Clare, Hugh's attractive sister, and Gerald. With the major characters, however, the representation of their subjective points of view illuminates their interrelationships. By entering the mind of Hugh immediately after we have read what Grace thinks about him (pp. 241—42), we can see the gap between their worlds and the limits of interpersonal communication.

In her next novel Rosamond Lehmann employs a narrative technique which is a combination of those of *Dusty Answer* and *A Note in Music*. *Invitation to the Waltz* is governed by the viewpoint of the central character, Olivia Curtis. It is occasionally complemented by her mother's, sister's, or brother's perspective at different moments, but it is Olivia's experience of two days in her life which provides the fabric of the story. The day of her seventeenth birthday and her first ball one week later are related in great detail. Such an account gives an impression of fulness of life, which is enhanced by Olivia's quickly changing moods and emotions. All the little preparations, every single encounter, are impressed on her mind and their significance is established by her private, individual hierarchy of values: an ill-cut dress becomes a disaster, a snub from a drunken boy an utter humiliation.

Olivia is living in an enchanted and exciting world of adolescence, with sudden premonitions of future disappointment (cf. p. 102), but for the most part in a state of receptive urgent expectation. This quality of her experience is rendered in the pace and tone of her internal comments throughout the novel.

[9] A. Hatcher, "Voir as a Modern Novelistic Device", *Philological Quarterly*, XXIII (1944), 373—74.

This is how Olivia thinks about the coming term without her sister, who is going away to Paris:

The afternoons would hold their mounting happiness. She would walk back to the station for the 4.45 quite strangled sometimes with happiness made up unaccountably of opalescent dusk in the streets, and lamplight, and soon the blossoming almond, the crocuses in the public gardens, and shapes of roof and chimney-pot cut on the sky, and the footsteps of quiet people going home, and the remembered voice of Monsieur Berton saying with tenderness: My favourite pupil, and a muddled feeling of the importance of intellectual things, a determination to excel in—in what?—in serious subjects, in literature, music. (pp. 65—66)

Furthermore, this quality of her experience is already suggested by the very tone of the novel's authorial opening; we are, as it were, dragged into the house of the Curtis family by some impatient family spirit:

The kettle's boiling, the cloth is spread, the windows are flung open. Come in, come in! Here dwells the familiar mystery. Come and find it! Each room is active, fecund, brimming over with it. The pulse beats. . . . Come and listen! (p. 4)

In keeping with Olivia's governing point of view is the choice of persons who are shown from the inside (James, Kate, Miss Robinson). They are always within Olivia's imaginative reach, whereas other characters, whom she does not know very well (the people at the dance), or whose experience is totally alien to hers (Uncle Oswald), are presented as Olivia *sees* them only. By largely limiting the point of view to Olivia, a sense of the intensity of her experience is conveyed.

The Weather in the Streets is a sequel to *Invitation to the Waltz*. The subject of the novel is Olivia's adulterous love affair with Rollo Spencer, and the centre of orientation is again Olivia, now ten years older. The affair is presented through the eyes of the totally involved Olivia, while Rollo is portrayed only from the outside. Other characters may talk about him (Lady Spencer, his sister Marigold), or treat him in a special way that exposes his social position, for example:

[The waiter] called Rollo "milord." Rollo said, "Hallo, you old villain," and it was an understood thing the bill was roughly double what it should be, and Rollo would put the pencil through the total and pay something quite different, though still enormous, (p. 163)

but we can see only such part of it as Olivia herself witnesses. This limitation of the point of view to the narrator-agent[10] gives intimacy to the treatment of the affair, restricting at the same time the moral scope and implications of the novel to Olivia's horizons.

One of the early reviewers of the book said that *The Weather in the Streets* is "based upon the assumption that even for certain intelligent, sophisticated persons love can become the most important thing in the world,

---

[10] Booth, pp. 153—54.

and upon the further assumption that the novelist may write about the passion of such persons in such a manner as to accept it at their own valuation."[11] This manner consists here in a special handling of the limited point of view. Olivia's disappointment in love, her "lack of belief", and her ultimate defeat (cf. below p. 124) are not set against any alternative moral framework. The "life of belief", as embodied by Mrs. Curtis or Olivia's friend Jocelyn, is not presented as a meaningful possibility for Olivia. There is an almost total identification between her perspective as the governing consciousness and as the main character. Her mood always determines the tone of a given passage. It was different in the *Invitation to the Waltz*, where Olivia's profound consternation and distress could at times produce comical effects (for example in the scene with George, where Olivia for a long time does not realize that his question "Were you out to-day?" referred to hunting, see p. 209). In *The Weather in the Streets* this identification is particularly strong in Part II, which is related in the first person. In Parts I, III, and IV there appear several excursions into the minds of some secondary characters: Olivia's sister, their parents. These passages are functional as a part of her background and throw some light on Olivia as seen by her family. In Part IV attention is shifted from Olivia's love affair to her friend Simon's death. This shift of interest and, though brief, of the centre of orientation from Olivia to Mrs. Cunningham, one of her friends, creates an effect of the passage of time. When, in the next section of the book, Olivia meets Rollo for the last time, it is by way of an epilogue for her, and she is disconcerted to find how differently Rollo looks at their relationship. On the whole the very short passages where we see Olivia's world with another character's eyes hardly affect the integrity of presentation of her private experience.

In *The Ballad and the Source* the treatment of the limited point of view is more involved than in any other novel of Rosamond Lehmann's. Here one character, Mrs. Jardine, is presented from the viewpoint of several people who have all been, in one way or another, attached to her at different phases of her life. There is Tilly, an old Cockney maid of Rebecca's grandmother; Maisie, Mrs. Jardine's granddaughter; Rebecca's parents; Auntie Mack, a relative of Maisie's father; Gil, a young sculptor and a close friend of Mrs. Jardine. Their views of Mrs. Jardine are sometimes contradictory: according to Tilly, who knew Mrs. Jardine in her youth, she was stubborn, proud and inconsiderate. For Auntie Mack she embodied goodness and consideration. Gil and Rebecca love her and feel that Mrs. Jardine cares for truth. Maisie, who as a child was brought up to hate her, says: "She knows a lot when she's at her best. When she's not on the prowl, she can be grand" (pp. 229—30).

[11] Joseph Wood Krutch, "All for Love", *The Nation*, CXLII (June 3, 1936), 713.

The story is related as it revealed itself to the child Rebecca and is told by her as an adult. When Rebecca was a young girl of ten, Mrs. Jardine confided in her and thus we have yet another perspective: Mrs. Jardine's own version of the story of her life as she strove to impart it to her eager listener. In James's phrase, we are "watching her, as it were, through the successive windows of other people's interest in her".[12] These people are all, to a certain extent, Jamesian *ficelles* whose primary function is to reveal different aspects of Mrs. Jardine's personality. James defines them as belonging "less to my subject than to my treatment of it".[13] Such a way of presentation—through the limited perspective of several outsiders—of the main character is in many ways more advantageous than the first person narrative, or "objective" third person narrative, could ever be. It gives an air of life-like ambiguity and adds to the depth of the portrayal of the main character.

On the publication of this novel Rosamond Lehmann was immediately acclaimed as "one of the James girls", and a reviewer exclaimed:

how Henry James would have been thrilled by this thing; but Henry could never have done the miracle she has achieved. How Edith Wharton would have been thrilled by it, too. Joseph Conrad would have relished with amazement the way this book is written.[14]

It is true that in her use of the limited point of view of Rebecca the book is extraordinarily Jamesian, reminding one in particular of *What Maisie Knew*. James saw interesting possibilities in Maisie's story in which the girl herself would be the "register of impressions".[15] He sketched his design as consisting in an attempt "to make and to keep her so limited consciousness the very field of my picture while at the same time guarding with care the integrity of the object represented."[16] He realized, however, the difficulty of achieving coherency and completeness and at the same time confining the picture only to what Maisie herself might be able to understand and formulate. Consequently, instead of restricting himself to the child's experience expressed in her own terms, he decided to give "the whole situation surrounding her, but . . . only through the occasions and connexions of her proximity and attention; only as it might pass before her and appeal to her."[17]

Rosamond Lehmann resorts to the same technique with a difference: whereas James amplifies the child's limited vision by his authorial remarks

---

[12] *The Art of the Novel,* p. 306.
[13] Ibid., p. 322.
[14] "One of the James Girls", *Newsweek,* XXV (April 9, 1945), 93.
[15] *What Maisie Knew,* preface, p. 2.
[16] Ibid., p. 5.
[17] Ibid., p. 6.

(for example: "[Maisie] waited ... while, between his big teeth, he [Beale] breathed the sighs she did n't know to be stupid"[18]), she introduces the grown-up Rebecca as the first-person narrator who faithfully restores her childhood memories and seldom accentuates her position as an adult. This occurs only sporadically, as when Rebecca evaluates her friendship with Maisie Thompson:

Maisie was the first woman friend I ever had. There were plenty of girls, then, and afterwards, with whom I played games and exchanged confidences, but my relationship with Maisie was so far removed from the waist-entwined, I've got a secret, giggle and whisper it, cross your heart you won't tell level that I think of it now as adult. (pp. 46—47)

A passage like this functions only as an aside in the main story, and the fact that the adult's vision does not influence Rebecca's early narration creates a greater suspense. As she avidly listens to the story of Mrs. Jardine, her interest is conveyed with a sense of its actuality and emotional immediacy. Suspense, apart from the story's being itself one of "crime and passion", is enhanced by Mrs. Jardine's remarkable style of expression and Tilly's dramatic talents:

"[...] you can't unplay the game that was played and never should'ave been." This doom-fraught speech, delivered with appropriate power, penetrated me like a probe, exploring depths that terrified me. With passionate reluctance, I insisted: "What did she do, Tilly?"
    I must have it, the worst, the Sin, straight out. But Tilly was creating drama. She had no intention of destroying her suspense to gratify a child's banal curiosity. She busied herself with the fur [...] looking haughty and malicious. Presently she thrust obliquely at her object, from a different angle. (p. 63)

The fact that the story is shown in the double perspective of the narrator *and* the listener makes for an objective distance, and phrases like "this doom-fraught speech", or "Tilly was creating drama", also have a distancing effect.

    In *The Ballad and the Source* the author is completely effaced since Rebecca is the narrator of the whole story. She is also involved in the story as one of the characters and, as she is merely an inexperienced girl, one gets the impression that the other characters, and particularly Mrs. Jardine,

must have created themselves. To some degree, all the unreliable narrators of modern literature, those of James and Ford and Conrad, accomplish the same end, in a roundabout manner; they provide a pole for the reader's natural desire to see who is telling the tale. Thus the characters in the tale achieve a factitious reality as the result of what amounts to an optical illusion.[19]

[18] Ibid., p. 138.
[19] E. L. Epstein, "The Irrelevant Narrator: A Stylistic Note on the Place of the Author in Contemporary Technique of the Novel", *Language and Style,* Winter 1969 (Southern Illinois Univ.), 93.

The first person narration creates the need to account for all the information Rebecca receives and thus we see her eavesdropping, reading her mother's letters (p. 216), and pretending false innocence in order to learn more and to satisfy her curiosity and "detective instinct". Rebecca's view is of necessity restricted; she is trying to get to the "source", the truth about Mrs. Jardine, but what she can get at is only the "ballad": a many-faceted image of a complex personality.

Rebecca's fresh perspective is due to her innocence and naivety, and these very qualities allow her to look at Mrs. Jardine with not too strongly preconceived moral ideas. She is only an unsuspecting child and, when she learns, for example, that Mrs. Jardine's daughter's guardian was a clergyman, her first thought is: "Then surely it must be all right this time. This at least must be a good man" (p. 127). Yet, though she does not make much of Mrs. Jardine's description of the man, she is nevertheless able to detect irony and malice in her voice. Still, her fundamental lack of ethical bias gives a particular objectivity to various situations which, had she the critical sense of an adult, she would not be able to view with the same candour: she would have to judge Mrs. Jardine (in a case like her attempt to "wean" her daughter Ianthe from her guardian by sending to her her own lover Paul) instead of listening only, with childish excitement, always loyal to Mrs. Jardine and ready to suspend her disbelief:

As if all were still happening, could yet be changed, as if now, this moment, the half-visionary figure was being devilishly threatened and deprived, I fought with passion to justify her, to give her her own. (p. 75)

Rebecca is often unaware of the significance of different facts and interprets them on the level appropriate to her age. The limitations of her understanding are often pointed out. They can create comical effects, as when Tilly says of Mr. Herbert, Mrs. Jardine's first husband:

"[...] 'e was better furnished in the top storey than 'e was elsewhere ..." [and Rebecca] wrestled fruitlessly to attach nameless implications to a whirling composite picture of wardrobes, chairs, tables, beds, and, at the very tip-top of a perpendicular staircase, one well-set-up gentleman tinkling with china fingers on the harpsichord. (p. 64)

Sometimes certain aspects of Mrs. Jardine's personality are explained to Rebecca by other persons (see Gil's comments, p. 240), but on the whole their views are far more biased than hers. Both Tilly and, up to a point, Maisie, are prejudiced against Mrs. Jardine, and their animosity obviously tinges their versions of the story, which are naturally inconsistent with Mrs. Jardine's own consciously woven heroic "ballad" about herself. Gradually, however, the story pieces itself together and Rebecca's knowledge, though by no means complete, transcends that of some of her informants. She knows, for instance why Ianthe used to sing German songs which bewildered her daughter Maisie. Yet Rebecca's privileged position is kept within the bounds of possibility: she is merely the one among the characters in the book whom we get to know most intimately from within, whereas all the others owe their reality to their contact with her. Rebecca compiles their partial points of view and, without passing judgements or challenging Mrs. Jardine's conduct, seeks to arrive at a complex and elusive truth. But she is far more than a compiler of different views; her own innocence and freshness create a special aura around the main heroine. The nature of Rebecca's personal interest, reflected in her point of view, is responsible for the particular vitality of the portrait of Mrs. Jardine.

The Echoing Grove recounts the story of a marital triangle for the most part from the viewpoint of all the three persons involved: Rickie Masters, his wife Madeleine, and her sister Dinah. There is also an undramatized narrator, whose function is to connect all the internal monologues and provide some external information (for example, about Dinah's finances, p. 18)[20] which, however, is not essential to the main concern of the novel: a representation of the anguish of love. Apart from the three principal characters, we enter now and then the minds of some minor characters, whose view of the protagonists contributes to the central theme but who are not at all developed as persons in their own right (see, for example, Mary Wainwright, p. 65). Georgie Worthington, despite the inner view treatment and the part she plays in Rickie's life, seems to be there as yet another commentator on his character, without much life of her own. But even Rickie, Madeleine and Dinah are shown chiefly in one aspect only: their love relations. This concentration is so strong that the book seems to be less concerned with individual, fully realized, characters than with different aspects of love itself.

This impression may be confirmed by the apparently erratic logic of the shifts of the point of view: for example, Part II begins with Dinah lying sleepless in bed at her sister's house, on the first night after their reconciliation brought about after fifteen years of estrangement. She is thinking about the room, Madeleine's taste in decorating, her niece Clarissa, her own baby born dead years ago. This leads her thoughts to the last time she saw Rickie: he was in a hurry because his wife expected him and they were going out to a party. The party is described from the viewpoint of Rickie and Madeleine and then, in the middle of the account, the narrator tells us how the party was remembered after many years by Rickie's friends, when he was already dead. One of those friends, Jack Worthington, thinks about Georgie, his future wife, and about her views on Rickie's marriage to Madeleine. From there we go back to the party itself, to Rickie's

[20] *The Echoing Grove* (London: Collins, 1953). All subsequent references are to this edition.

conversation with Georgie, and to Madeleine's inner view of the rest of the dance, blended with an objective outside perspective (and Mary Wainwright's impressions) of Rickie's strange condition. Next there is Madeleine's view of the scene after the party with Rickie at home. It was the night of Clarissa's conception; in a few sentences we are told about Madeleine's pregnancy. Then Rickie, on the night of Clarissa's birth, thinks of the other child, Dinah's. At this point the circle is completed: we are brought back to their stillborn baby. The whole story of Rickie's relationship with Dinah unfolds itself before his mind (again with glimpses into Madeleine's consciousness), back to the very beginning.

Such an order of events (and it is similar in Parts III and IV) gives a fragmentary picture of the characters but in return a relatively complete presentation of the beginning, development and end of the complicated love affair. The multiplicity of subjective and limited points of view serves to bring out a certain objective reality: the reality of an interpersonal relationship.

2. Time Patterns

Just as the subjective vision of life implied the limited point of view, with its selection of experience significant to the observer-narrator, it also presupposes a particular treatment of time. The importance of the time factor in fiction has been emphasized by A. A. Mendilow, who in his book *Time and the Novel* (1952) claims that

the time element in fiction is of major importance, that in a large measure it determines the author's choice and treatment of his subject, the way he articulates and arranges the elements of his narrative, and the way he uses language to express his sense of the process and meaning of living.[1]

And indeed, it can be seen that the presentation of a character through the limited point of view involves a specific handling of time in accordance with its subjective perception by the individual. Such a treatment of time necessarily affects the structure of the novels.

Generally speaking, the novels of Rosamond Lehmann show the frequent tendency of much modern fiction to transfer the events described from the outer world of action to the inner world of thought and emotion. What matters most are the thoughts and feelings rather than the actions of Judith (*Dusty Answer*), Grace Fairfax (*A Note in Music*), Olivia Curtis (*Invitation to the Waltz* and *The Weather in the Streets*) or Madeleine (*The Echoing Grove*). This turning inward is of fundamental importance to the treatment of time by

[1] A. A. Mendilow, *Time and the Novel* (New York: Humanities Press, 1972), p. 234.

41

the novelist, and it is closely connected with the impact of depth psychology on the modern novel. The interest in the semi- and subconscious levels of personality, the association processes, the working of the mind on the border of sleep, are central to such novels as *The Echoing Grove*. Psychoanalysis is also an expressed interest of Rosamond Lehmann's adult heroines whose sensibilities set the tone of the novels (for example, Olivia in *The Weather in the Streets* speaks jestingly of "sublimating her bath-lust" which is an act of "back to the womb with a vengeance", p. 216).

The traditional chronological sequence is not adequate "in the evocation of mental processes where associative memory follows purely private and individual laws of sequence."[2] Therefore the modern psychological novel tends, in varying degree, to disregard external continuity and to progress rather through the revealing moments significant to the characters' inner life. And so the novels of Rosamond Lehmann (especially after *Dusty Answer*) lack epic completeness; instead, in the manner of lyrical poetry, they focus on short periods of emotional intensity: *A Note in Music*, for example, offers an exhaustive description of a few days which are significant subjectively and the plot is practically reduced to these occasions.

On a purely psychological plane time cannot be measured by the clock but rather by the individual experience of duration. This is bound to vary not only from one character to another, but also within the awareness of one consciousness, since "interior time [is] estimated by constantly varying values."[3] In *A Note in Music* the period of Hugh Miller's stay in the town was to him just another tedious year of an unsuccessful attempt to settle down to work, while to Grace Fairfax it was, in the emotional sphere, the most vivid period since her early youth. In *Dusty Answer,* the three formative years at college seemed to Judith Earle insignificant and wiped out the moment she left Cambridge.

In Rosamond Lehmann's novels, however, the irregular sequence of inner thoughts and feelings does not wholly replace causality on the plane of exterior action (as happens in some novels of Virginia Woolf). The inner and outer durations are mingled in different proportions. *Dusty Answer* is the most traditional of her novels in its treatment of time. It plunges *in medias res*, then goes back and digressions in the form of Judith's memories establish the background that provides an exposition of the present situation, and then the narration proceeds in chronological order to the end. *A Note in Music* follows the thoughts of several persons on a few days within one year and presents their past by means of flashbacks, stream of consciousness and associations started off by the present situation. In all her subsequent novels Rosamond Lehmann makes use of these devices, until they culminate in her

---

[2] Ibid., p. 75.
[3] Ibid., p. 118.

last novel, *The Echoing Grove*, where all significant events are irrevocably past and exist only in the consciousness of the characters. They are related as they derive from the present thoughts of Madeleine and Dinah, in the order they come to their minds by the principle of association. When Madeleine, half-awake, thinks of her children, it brings to her mind her lover Jocelyn, introduced to her by her son. The thought of her unfaithfulness makes her think of her husband, and so on.

No totally "objective" recapitulation of the past is possible: it is always charged emotionally and directed by the subsequent event from which it acquires its meaning. The perspective of the observer-narrator is influenced by his position in time in relation to the action recounted. We can speak of two time perspectives: one is from the point of the action just being unfolded, where a sense of "presentness" is conveyed (the first meeting of Rollo and Olivia in *The Weather in the Streets*, the final scene between Judith and Roddy in *Dusty Answer,* the ball in *Invitation to the Waltz*, etc.). Although written in the past tense, it creates an impression of emotions as lived just now, or recorded immediately after. Another time perspective is from the point of some present time in relation to which the events described belong to the past (Part II of *The Weather in the Streets,* the story of Mrs. Jardine in *The Ballad and the Source,* the love triangle in *The Echoing Grove*) and are evaluated in the light of the present.

When events from the past are brought in, the modern novel often exploits the structural possibilities of the film, with its disregard for chronological order. The most common device is perhaps the time shift, of which there are many examples in Rosamond Lehmann. *The Echoing Grove* consists entirely of such "jumps" in time which are highly significant for the story's presentation. Jonathan Raban called "this flexibility ... one of the novelist's major instruments: he can indicate the relative value of each occurrence by his handling of pace."[4]

The narration in the novels of Rosamond Lehmann is often characterized by time shifts from the "now" of the action: in *Dusty Answer* the whole of

---

[4] Jonathan Raban, *The Techniques of Modern Fiction* (London: Notre Dame Univ. Press, 1969), p. 57.

Other such film devices are: angle of vision (as when Judith in *Dusty Answer* is watching the cousins at night from her observation point by a willow stump in the river, herself unnoticed, see p. 54); flash-backs (for example, in *The Weather in the Streets,* Olivia's recollection of her affair with Rollo, as she is travelling by train from Austria back to England); close-ups (Rebecca's first meeting with Mrs. Jardine in *The Ballad and the Source,* p. 10). The film language is even used at one point by Dinah in *The Echoing Grove*:

> Everything looked expectant, supercharged, dramatic: opening shots in a French film, camera turning on doors, pavements, lamp-post [...] sound track picking up the thin invisible piano, the screech of a rusty wheel, shouts, motor horns and running footsteps [...] When will they move, that pair of lovers? What are they muttering, their lips stiff,

Part I is written from the point of view of the eighteen-year old Judith, who goes back and away from her "now" which is picked up again in Part II and thence followed chronologically. In *The Ballad and the Source* the story of Mrs. Jardine starts relatively close to the end, when she is already an old woman, then it moves one step backwards (through Maisie's narration) to the times of Ianthe's family life, next it goes further back (Tilly's relation) to the young days of Sibyl Jardine to proceed (through various narrators) closer and closer to the denouement which takes place in the late summer of 1914 and is told to Rebecca at Christmas 1916. This is the order in which Rebecca became acquainted with the story.

In *The Echoing Grove* the time shift is not merely a way of introducing the expository information: it is essential to the building of the book's complex structure. The novel consists of five time sections: "Afternoon", "Morning", "Nightfall", "Midnight", and "Early Hours", each corresponding to the time of a character's reminescences. The story is revealed as it passes through the minds of the protagonists, or rather as it is re-lived by them, not from the beginning to the end, but through the key moments that imprinted themselves most powerfully in their memories: Madeleine's discovery of her husband's and sister's affair, the quarrels and breaks and reconciliations, the last meeting of Dinah and Rickie, their last holiday together, Rickie's death. It produces an effect similar to the processing of a film: each consciousness is like a different solution, and by the end of the book the picture is completed through the sum of all the reminiscences. The presentation of an event through different centres of orientation gives new meaning to it and its reappearance in time adds a new quality: Rickie's cuff-links become in this way a recurring motif in the novel. Like other elements existing in the memories of several people, they add coherence to the presented world.

In *Dusty Answer* Judith's childhood is foreshortened when she views it from her present point in time. She recalls the occasions which are both pertaining to her present mood and representative of the past. Similarly in *The Weather in the Streets,* when Olivia is thinking about the happy phase of her affair with Rollo, a number of similar situations coalesce in her mind into one, so that one telephone conversation, for example, stands for the typical one:

"Look here." He always said that on the telephone. "What are you doing to-night?" He was always guarded on the telephone, crisp, off-hand, he never spoke for long—only to make quick arrangements. He never said anything nice. (p. 145)

looking hard at one another, then away? She wears her hair shoulder-length, rolled under, she wears a mackintosh and carries a shabby suitcase: clearly she is the heroine. (p. 44)

Dinah watches herself and Rickie from the outside, as if on the screen where one cannot influence the action.

This is the time perspective "past-oriented", where the events described are viewed from a distance. More frequent, however, is the situation when the past is presented as if it were another present, with no radical difference from the "now" which, after all, is also rendered in the past tense. A. A. Mendilow explains this phenomenon in the following manner:

the reader feels the past of the novel as present, even if he is familiar with the story, or has read it before, because he transfers to himself the absence in the minds of the characters of the sense of familiarity which ... is one of the elements that gives rise to the idea of pastness.[5]

It is possible, however, to convey an effect of the presentness of an event that is already past in the mind of a character, as when Olivia, after many months, thinks about her first rendezvous with Rollo:

Twenty-past ten, and a car came round into the street and stopped, and next moment the bell rang. Starting up weak in the bowels from waiting, starting downstairs in a flurry, then making myself go slow, in a calm way, opening—and there he was on the doorstep. (p. 148)

Such a sense of a situation as taking place now creates a dramatic effect and, through suspense, increases the pace of narration. Conversely, when a character in the novel experiences the flow of time as slow, or views it from a later perspective (Part I of *Dusty Answer*, the greater portion of *The Echoing Grove*), an effect of the passage of time is created.

Since the time perspective is personal, the events brought to the fore are significant of the present preoccupations of the characters and reflect only those aspects of their past lives which are still important parts of their "now", with whole areas of their background omitted. Yet the past is an integral part of the present which, "like a note in music, is nothing but as it appertains to what is past and what is to come" (W. S. Landor, the epigraph to *A Note in Music*). Behind such a conception of time, characteristic of much modern literature, lies the extremely influential Bergsonian theory of *durée*, which describes time as an indivisible flow,[6] a continuous movement that cannot be rationally measured but only grasped intuitively. The effects of Bergson's ideas on art have been frequently discussed. A. A. Mendilow wrote that Bergson's theory "has brought about a new conception of character in much modern fiction, especially in the stream of consciousness novel. The fixing of personality by external description, by labels and definitions and lists of characteristics has been discarded as false. ... The theory of *durée* has similarly led to a new conception of plot and structure. It has suggested the progressive narrowing of the fictional duration covered by the novel at the same time as the expansion of the psychological duration of

[5] Mendilow, p. 98.
[6] Susanne Langer, *Feeling and Form: A Theory of Art* (New York: Scribner, 1953), pp. 112–15.

the characters."[7] And thus, although the chronological duration of some of Rosamond Lehmann's novels is restricted to a few days only, the areas of time actually covered are much greater.

A Note in Music can serve as an example here: the action of the novel begins in January and ends about a year later, covering the time of Hugh Miller's stay in the town. Each of the book's seven episode-parts covers one day, five of which contain Grace's only encounters with Hugh. Outwardly not much happens on these occasions: Grace's husband Tom points Hugh out to her in a cinema; three weeks later Norah and Grace give Hugh a lift and they have tea in Grace's house. The next time Hugh stops to chat with Grace for a few minutes in the park. The following day all of them—Hugh, Clare, Norah, Gerald and Grace—drive out for a picnic. The next part describes Grace's extraordinary, lonely and sadly happy holiday in the country, and an August fair in town at which Pansy meets first Hugh and then Tom. At the end of September, Hugh calls on Grace to say good-bye. The last episode is an autumnal epilogue: there is no more Hugh and everything has apparently gone back to normal.

The two main characters, Grace and Norah, unable to find a meaningful continuity in their lives, resignedly turn backwards from the emptiness and dullnes of their "now". To Norah,

there came now and then—at a sound, a scent, a word—intimations from the past; live threads waver out, throwing feelers after hints of affinity [. . .] striving to shape the spiritual shape of what has been; till it seems in a moment all will be linked, gathered up into unity and purpose. And the moment does not come [. . .] (p. 77)

This domination of the characters' subjective experience of time is reflected in the narrative technique of the novel. Interior monologue, indirect third-person stream of consciousness and memory digression adequately convey the changing states of mind of Grace and other characters. The main personages emerge in full despite the fact that the novel covers only a small number of short periods of time (usually one day) scattered at varying intervals within one year. The past, which plays such an important role both in the awareness of the characters and in the novel's composition, is depicted best by means of the technique of the subjective point of view. It "conveys directness of presentation and immediacy because it resembles the way people react in real life. We do not see ourselves as others see us. We are aware of the whole pressure of the past on our present, of the tug and clash of forces that may or may not express themselves in terms of action."[8]

In *A Note in Music*, as in many modern novels, the exposition of the characters is interwoven with the main action taking part in the "now". This exposition takes the form of recollections and associations which derive from

---

[7] Mendilow, pp. 149—50.
[8] Ibid., p. 114.

the present situation and at the same time, by enriching it, modify it. Part I of *A Note in Music* begins with Grace dressing for dinner, which she is to have with her husband. She can hear him from her room, singing in his bath, and it makes her think of her father, who years ago used to sing the same song; then her mind wanders to Tom himself, his character, their marriage. Doing her hair, she thinks about her appearance and why she stopped caring about it: that she was unhappy, had grown indifferent. She remembers her moments of happiness, when, long ago, she looked after a mongrel puppy. But it died and she took it "for a sign that nothing would ever come right for her" again (p. 8), and this was even worse than when her baby was born dead afterwards. Various thoughts flit through her mind, and by the time she is ready to go down to dinner, the reader knows her intimately. This erratic chain of associations introduces not only Grace and the circumstances of her life, but also Tom and their relationship from her point of view. The intermingling of the past with the present promotes the effect of in-depth creation of the character whose individual sense of life is communicated through the temporal dimension.

Four of Rosamond Lehmann's six novels are constructed around the experience of love and its different phases. In *Dusty Answer* the subject of the story is the emotional involvement of Judith with the five Fyfe cousins. The novel deals with her memories of them as children and her encounters with them in later life, and it ends when Judith's urge to get to know and understand the cousins is spent. In *A Note in Music* Grace's love for Hugh stands in the centre of the novel, and the main characters' preoccupation with the passage and nature of time constitutes an important element. In *The Weather in the Streets* Olivia's affair with Rollo is followed from the beginning to its end. Time as experienced by people in love is described also in *The Echoing Grove*, which is an expansion of many of the themes treated before in *The Weather in the Streets*. In *The Echoing Grove* an entangled family situation lasting about twenty years is comprised within the framework of two days and nights. Like the other novels of Rosamond Lehmann, the book deals with a closed time unit. Here this is emphasized by the "circular" structure of the novel: we are presented with several personal variants of the same sequences of time, viewed from varying distances of years. The emphasis on the inward, individual experience contributes to the general effect of an intensely personal and subjective world.

3. Distance and Immediacy

Rosamond Lehmann's experimentation in the form and style of her novels is undoubtedly connected with their "inwardness", which presupposes a precise and individual medium, since, in the words of David Daiches, "the communication of a private world requires much more subtle technique than that of a public world."[1] In this section certain stylistic devices will be examined which are employed by the novelist in her treatment of the limited point of view and the time element. I will concentrate on the handling of distance and immediacy, which is an aspect of her narrative technique that largely contributes to the effectiveness of the subjective vision of life in the novels.

The limited point of view in the novels of Rosamond Lehmann is, on the level of language, rendered by the predominant use of third person narration, interchanging occasionally with the first person. The only exception here is *The Ballad and the Source,* which employs first person narration throughout. It is in the alternations between these two manners of narrative that the handling of distance between the reader and the narrator-observer lies. The diminishing of this distance, as well as of the distance between the narrator and the depicted world, is one of the major factors responsible for the creating of a subjective, inward-centred vision of life.

It is interesting to observe how the fluctuations between the first, third, and sometimes second person modify the distance between the character's experience and the reader. First person narration, disparaged by Henry James as bound to lead to looseness of construction,[2] has the power of intensifying a character's experience as well as of heightening the effect of authenticity by the complete withdrawal of the authorial commentary. This is how it functions in *The Weather in the Streets,* where the use of the first person is perhaps most varied. In Part I of the novel, it is reserved for the thoughts of Olivia, while the outward actions are described in the third person, with the transfer often taking place within one sentence. For example: "She stopped [...] choked by the usual struggle of conflicting impulses: to explain, to say nothing; to trust, to be suspicious [...] to let nobody come too near me" (p. 18). Similar combinations of the first and the third person are frequent also in Parts III and IV of the book: "But when they got upstairs he loosened his arm, her hand dropped down ... or I took it away" (p. 317).

Part II, however, is written in the first person throughout. It is Olivia's recollection of the first phase of her affair with Rollo Spencer, as she is falling asleep on a train from Austria to England. Although Olivia is looking back on the past period of eight months, it acquires a peculiar feverish vividness in her mind because she is worried, tired and sick, and somehow suspended in a "no man's land"—alone on a train at night. The immediacy brought about by the use of the first person is greatly enhanced by the

[1] Daiches, *The Novel and the Modern World,* p. 10.
[2] Henry James, *The Art of the Novel,* p. 320.

spontaneous order of short sentences which, although fully comprehensible, are reminiscent of the thought processes:

I did try to write now and then, I got about half a sketch done, but I kept losing my way in it; and the listening and waiting interfered. A person in my state can't work. . . . Oh! Sometimes I wish . . . no . . . yes, sometimes I wish I could be free again, able to belong to myself. (pp. 202—203)

The use of the first person for the most intense phase of the relationship sets this period apart, and Olivia's purely subjective awareness of it stands in the centre.

The habitual manner of mixing the first and the third person in the narration of the rest of the novel sometimes makes for a blurred borderline between the undramatized narrator (see above, p. 33 note 8) and the narrator-agent (see above, p. 35 note 10). The line is still less clear when the point of view is moving from one consciousness to another, as it occasionally does in *The Weather in the Streets*. During a family dinner Olivia is thinking:

And after that I'll ask for details of Miss Robinson's complete breakdown. . . . And after that. . . .
Across the table they began to ply a peaceful shuttle between the three of them, renewing, re-inforcing, patching over rents and frayed places with old serviceable thread. They were tough still; they were a family. That which had chanced to tie them all up together from the start persisted, irrevocably, far below consciousness, far beyond the divergences of the present, uniting them in a mysterious reality, independent of reason. As it was in the beginning, is now. . . . Only the vast central lighting-piece no longer stupefied the cloth with a white china glare. When the daughters came home, grown up to have ideas on becoming lighting, they condemned it [. . .] (pp. 59—60)

It is only with the last sentence that we realize these are Olivia's mother's thoughts. The preceding four sentences, beginning with "Across the table . . .", may be read either as Olivia's or the undramatized narrator's reflections, and even Mrs. Curtis cannot be excluded. The distance between the mother and the daughter diminishes and the effect of the subconscious tie between them is conveyed, but the situation is not clear. All the time, however, the reader finds himself in Olivia's own personal world where little beyond her subjective vision of experience is admitted. Yet an impression of objectivity is produced by the third person narration, and also by the reader's entering into the minds of other characters: in this way the reality of Olivia's world is established. Similar effects, *mutatis mutandis*, are achieved in the other novels.

But since third person narration is limited to the outward actions of Olivia and there is no evaluation of her conduct, her experience is presented entirely in terms of her moral and intellectual perspective. The authenticity of the first person novel is hardly affected despite the prevalent use of the third person.

49

We never for a moment know what Rollo thinks; it is always "He *seemed* pleased and amused" (p. 18), or "He turned towards her quickly, *as if* the use of his Christian name had moved him" (p. 24, italics mine). Even Olivia's appearance is introduced in a way similar to first person narration: "[Rollo] looked her over with a warm blue eye, and she saw an image of herself in his mind [...]" (p. 13). Similarly in *A Note in Music*, the only times we learn about Grace's appearance is when she looks at herself in the mirror (p. 5) or is watched by another character in the novel (p. 122). One can conclude from this technique that an "objective" view of character is not possible at all: we are always presented with somebody's impression of a situation (cf. above, pp. 28–29).

The author's direct description would obviously be unjustified when the narrative point of view is consistently restricted to the consciousness of a participant in the story. This necessity to exclude the author-narrator leads in *Dusty Answer* to a rather roundabout manner of commenting on Judith. During a conversation with Julian she feels sorry for him, realizing that

all his talking seemed less a normal exercise than a forced hysterical activity assumed to ease sharp wretchedness [...]
He flung round on the piano-stool and dropped his face into his hands, rubbing his eyes wearily.
"Julian—I wish you weren't—I wish you could—"
He looked up, startled, saw her expression, looked quickly away again and gave an embarassed laugh like a boy. (pp. 71–72)

That last sentence tells the reader about Judith's appearance indirectly, through the impression she makes on Julian, which is conveyed clearly without departing from her perspective on the situation.

The fact that the cousins are shown only in their relation with Judith strongly affects the distance between the reader and these characters: they become one degree more remote and the detachment increases when Judith herself experiences them as remote and unreal. And thus, when they leave for good the first time, "being alone came again as the natural stuff of life, and the children next door were gone and lost, as if they had never been" (p. 26). Similarly, they grow dim and unreal when Judith goes to college. Every time they reappear in her life, often after intervals of many years, they are easily recognizable, since they stay basically the same, although Judith's understanding of them grows. Every time she approaches the cousins, full of curiosity and expectation, and waiting for them to reveal the heart of their "mystery", the expectations of the reader run parallel to Judith's and, with her, he sees them "objectively"—as strangers. Judith repeats what they say and reproduces their outer actions. In this manner we see them as one watches people in life: from the outside. At the same time we know both what Judith does and what she feels in her contacts with the other characters. Therefore our distance towards Judith vanishes: we no longer watch her, but rather watch with her; she is our medium and in this role her own reality becomes intensified.

In *Dusty Answer* there is also another manner of narration, for which the second person is used: that of the young child Judith whose way of looking at the world is preserved in the memories of the eighteen-year old Judith:

[Mariella] blew out her cheeks, stuffed a cushion in her knickers and strutted coarsely. That was irresistible. You had to squeal with laughter. After that the others came in rather quietly and were very polite [...] And after tea they asked her to choose the game. So everything was all right. (pp. 7—8)

The use of the second person ("you had to squeal with laughter") appears sometimes when Judith watches herself from a certain distance in time, or reflects with detachment, as for example: "Supposing you looked like Mabel, would you love beauty even more passionately, or be so jealous of it that you hated it?" (p. 132). As J. Raban observes, the second person pronoun serves "to forge an intimate link between author, character and reader".[3]

The second person pronoun, however, is used only occasionally, and the functions of the third person are more important. Third person narration, besides imparting a measure of solidity to the outer world, has one more advantage. It gives an aura of presentness, or what we may call "temporal" immediacy, to what we read, despite the fact that it is written in the past tense. Thus although the third person on the whole increases the "spatial" distance between the reader and the character (as opposed to first person narration), the same third person diminishes the "temporal" distance. A. A. Mendilow notices that there is

a vital difference between writing a story forward from the past, as in the third person novel, and writing it backward from the present, as in the first person novel. Though both are equally written in the past, in the former the illusion is created that the action is taking place; in the latter, the action is felt as having taken place.[4]

When we read:

His eyes travelled intently over her and he smiled to himself. She looked up at him. Yes, all was well. For this evening some illusion was being breathed out, some reflection thrown back of a power as mystic, as capricious in its comings and goings as it was recognizable when it came. No need for anxiety now: it would carry her through. I shall enjoy myself. (*The Weather in the Streets*, pp. 67—68)

an illusion of the presentness of the action is created since we, like Olivia, do not know what the party will be like. If the second sentence in this excerpt read "I looked up at him", we would automatically assume that Olivia is remembering the occasion at some later point in the future. The next three sentences are written in *erlebte Rede*[5], an intermediate form between direct

[3] Raban, p. 30.
[4] Mendilow, p. 107.
[5] This discussion of *erlebte Rede* is based on Staffan Björck's *Romanens formvärld: Studier i*

51

and indirect speech. In *erlebte Rede* the past tense of the narration and the third person are preserved but, by omitting the words "Olivia thought", the distance between her and the reader is diminished. *Erlebte Rede* provides both a more intimate and a more dynamic formulation of the character's thoughts than indirect speech. It functions in this passage as an intermediate form between the third person of reported thought and the first person of the direct speech in the last sentence. "I shall enjoy myself" places us in the "now" of Olivia's expectation.

The Ballad and the Source is a case of skilful handling of the temporal distance. The reader is most of the time aware of the double perspective of the various narrators combined with that of Rebecca-the listener (cf. above, p. 36—37). Thus we know more about the way Mrs. Jardine was perceived by the other characters at different times (especially Rebecca) than what she was actually like. The occasional appearance of the grown-up Rebecca emphasizes the distance from the story, which was told to Rebecca as a child and a young girl but actually took place chiefly in the even more remote past. The presentation of Mrs. Jardine from varying distances heightens the impression of the elusiveness of a definite interpretation of her character. J. Raban mentions this connection between the shifting in time and the reader's distance from the story: "Most narratives mix their tenses: some parts occur in the distant past while some survive into the present, so that the reader is held in a flexible relationship with the events of the story, sometimes involved, sometimes detached."[6]

The modifications of temporal distance in the novels of Rosamond Lehmann play an important part in her depiction of the continuity of the past with the present in the lives of her characters. In *A Note in Music* the past comes to Grace in sudden flashes of memory released by a sight or a sound (p. 1). Its vitality and glamour serve as a foil to the dullness of her present life. As for *The Echoing Grove*, its action proper takes place many years before the book's present time of reconciliation between the two sisters, and one of the novel's main concerns is an exploration of the meaning of this past in their lives, which are unavoidably a sum of their past experiences (cf. above, p. 44).

The shifting of the temporal distance is most often brought about through entering the minds of the characters in the form of their memory-digressions. Sometimes, however, it is achieved by means of dialogue, which has the power of bringing nearer the events of the past (and past in the fictional time of the novel too), so that we read them with a sense of their actuality, although they may be long past from the point of view of the "now" of the hero. We may take an example from *Dusty Answer*, where dialogue

prosaberättarens teknik (Stockholm: Natur och Kultur, 1969), pp. 120—27, 159—65.
[6] Raban, p. 24.

constitutes the main narrative technique and where there is scarcely a page without it in the whole novel. Part I of the book is written from the point of view of Judith awaiting the return of her childhood companions. She remembers them in a sequence of little scenes whose presentness is reinforced by the fact that the conversations from childhood are merely repeated (together with the child Judith's feelings) and not commented on by the older Judith who recollects them:

> Another time [Charlie] took a pin out of his coat and said:
> "D'you see what this is?"
> "A pin."
> "Guess where I found it."
> "In the seat of your chair."
> The flippancy was misplaced. He ignored it and said impressively:
> "In my pudding at school."
> "Oh!"
> "I nearly swallowed it."
> "*Oh!*"
> "If I had I'd 'a' died."
> He stared at her.
> "Oh, *Charlie!* ... "
> "You can keep it if you like."
> He was so beautiful, so gracious, so munificient that words failed. ...
> She put the pin in a sealed envelope and wrote on it, "The pin that nearly killed D. F." with the date; and laid it away in the wash-stand drawer with her will [...] After that she was a good deal encouraged to hope he might marry her. (pp. 13—14)

This incident from the past helps to recreate Judith's background for the reader: it is functional as a part of the exposition. At the same time it is an integral part of Judith's character in the sense that it is re-lived by her as actual: "the past is felt not as distinct from the present but included in it and permeating it."[7]

Another way of creating temporal immediacy—besides third person narration as described above and the self-evident presentness of present tense narration which, however, cannot be sustained for long—is the use of elliptical sentences. They are extremely frequent in Rosamond Lehmann's novels and, combined with *erlebte Rede* and direct speech in dialogues, are an effective means of quickening the pace of the novel and positioning the reader "inside" the narrator-agent's experience:

> Nibbling a biscuit. ... Around me the furniture frozen into night silence, friendly, estranged. ... Kate, Mother, Dad, the maids asleep upstairs [...] My own bedroom waiting, awake for me. ... Peep in on Kate. Then a hot bath: float in water, warm water, softly dissolve; without one thought sink into sleep.
>
> (*The Weather in the Streets,* p. 136)

---

[7] Mendilow, p. 104.

or:

Late afternoon, moon-coloured street-and-roofscape [...] spectral sky, green-tinged, an air he drank as he ran—ice water laced with fire; afternoon of a Friday, Madeleine gone to the country with the children (whooping cough convalescence) and not expecting him: God on his side as usual. [...] But once an inky night had fallen, once well out on the first long lap to the south-west, and unable to make speed on the tricky though sanded roads—then he had time to reflect.

(*The Echoing Grove*, p. 92)

In both passages the elliptical sentences of interior monologue dissolve the distance between the reader and the characters. Passages of this kind occur in all the six novels. Their effectiveness lies not only in the shortening and incompleteness of sentences (which has come to be accepted in fiction as the more realistic way of presenting consciousness) but also in the lack of a mediator between the reader and the consciousness of the character. It is different when we read: "Olivia burst suddenly into a loud vulgar chuckle" (*The Weather in the Streets*, p. 49)—the author's intervention places us outside Olivia's mind as observers.

Intensity of experience also accounts for the effect of immediacy. Rosamond Lehmann often conveys it by means of words and phrases evoking concrete sensations and images. This is the very beginning of the ball for Olivia and her sister Kate in *Invitation to the Waltz*:

From the sanctuary of the bedroom, from thick rugs, whispering voices, soft lights and mirrors, four-poster strewn with wraps of velvet, fur, brocade, they emerged—crying in their hearts: Wait! Wait!—wishing to draw back, to hide; wishing to plunge on quickly now, and be lost, be mingled. (p. 153)

The broken syntax of this passage is instrumental in reproducing the dynamics of Olivia's perception. Rosamond Lehmann is concerned here with an accurate rendering of the "feel" of experience and the atmosphere as it is apprehended by her characters. The significance of an event is determined by its impact on a character's mind; the novelist represents mental states and feelings in which trivial things are also included and thus a particular impression of intimacy is formed. Olivia and Kate are taken to the ball in a taxi:

They went out into the damp and starless night, walking gingerly in their new slippers. Then the smell, sour, thick, of Walker's taxi enveloped them in its familiar exciting prelude. His hairy tickling rug was tucked around them [...] (p. 150)

In this short passage an atmosphere of intimacy is created through the reference to the world of the senses as experienced by Olivia. Penetrating descriptions of sensory perceptions enhance the subjective quality of Rosamond Lehmann's prose, which as a rule shows a great sensitivity to the physical qualities of things: their colour, texture, smell and touch. The style is sensuous and lyrical, as in a typical passage from *The Weather in the Streets*:

away from London. Lentil, saffron, fawn were left behind. A grubby jaeger shroud lay over the first suburbs; but then the woollen day clarified, and hoardings, factory buildings, the canal with its barges, the white-boled orchards, the cattle and willows and flat green fields loomed secretively, enclosed within the transparency like drenched indigo muslin. (p. 10)

And another example from *Dusty Answer*:

The Indian summer stretched out through October that year. The closing harmonies were so complete that the gardens of the earth seemed to repeat and enrich the gardens of the sky; and a day like a sunflower broadened to a sunset of full dahlias and late roses; with clouds above them massed, burnished and edged with bloom like the foliage of the trees of earth. Slowly at night the chill mists, bittersweet in smell, luminous beneath the moon, crept over and blotted all out. (pp. 139–40)

The impressionistic character of these descriptions assists in bringing the reader closer to the characters' experience, thereby helping to decrease distance.

All the stylistic devices mentioned here which affect the handling of distance and immediacy—the alternations between the first and the third person narration, the consistent use of the restricted point of view, the occasional second person pronoun, *erlebte Rede*, the shifting of temporal distance, dialogue, elliptical sentences, the evocative and often lyrical style of the descriptions of the texture of perception—all these elements are significant in building a subjective vision of life.

Chapter III

Characterization

In Chapter II we considered the narrative technique in the novels of Rosamond Lehmann and observed how a subjective vision of life is created through the choice of the point of view and the resulting treatment of time, distance, and immediacy. Naturally these elements of fiction are expressed through character, since character is the basic concern of practically all novels. In order to show how the subjectivism of the presentation of the world in the novels is paralleled by the quality of human relationships, it may be helpful to examine first how Rosamond Lehmann creates her characters. Thus a link will be established between the methods (Chapter II) and the meanings of the novels (Chapter IV), since in discussing how the characters are drawn we shall simultaneously observe what they are like.

Section I, "Inner Monologue vs. Dramatic Scenes", is chiefly concerned with the implications of the limited point of view for characterization. Both the secondary characters and the protagonists in the novels are discussed as they reveal themselves internally—through their thoughts, feelings, and perceptions, and externally—in their actions and in dialogue.

Section 2, "Contrasting and Complementary Visions", discusses the role of the shifted point of view in characterization, especially the effects of the multiple point of view on the reader's perspective on the characters.

Section 3, "Repetition with Variation", analyses the time element in the creation of the character and his world.

1. Inner Monologue versus Dramatic Scenes

It seems obvious that the limited point of view must affect the ways of characterization open to the novelist. Since the picture of characters and events is mostly filtered through a consciousness within the novel, direct characterization by the author in his own right is virtually non-existent. Nonetheless it is naturally he who communicates the thoughts of his characters, and strives after dramatic representation of their mind processes. The old Jamesian precept of showing, not telling, a story is scrupulously followed by Rosamond Lehmann. At the same time her typically modern interest in inner motives and the subjective qualities of experience is, in my opinion, successfully balanced in the total portrayal of her characters by their "objective" aspect, as it reveals itself in their social interplay. A closer look at the manner in which the characters are created will show how this balance is achieved.

One of the most important implications of the limited point of view is that a character is both an object and a source of awareness for the reader. Not only is the consciousness of Judith Earle or Grace Fairfax the prism through which we view all or part of the action, but they also participate in it (see above, p. 30). A character functions as a source of awareness for the reader when his thoughts, emotions, and perceptions are revealed. This is achieved mainly by interior monologues. When the same character is shown in his other function, as taking part in the action, the dramatic techniques of fiction are employed. Almost any scene chosen at random from *Dusty Answer*, for example, may serve to illustrate this double role of the narrator-agent Judith:

> [Geraldine] leaned against the mantelpiece and, staring at Judith, flung at her: "What's all this about?"
> Judith sat down again, without a word, and waited, steadily holding the green eyes with her own. She heard the blood beat deafeningly in her ears [. . .] Judith thought, with a shudder of excitement and anguish: "Wait, wait. It is because you are not used to it that it seems like physical blows [. . .] Carry it off." [. . .]
> Geraldine took a gold cigarette-case and the amber holder from a gold chain bag with a sapphire clasp.
> "It's pretty awful, isn't it, to be so mean and petty? I'm sorry for you, I must say."
> "Please don't be sorry for me." She noted her own voice, icy and polite. (p. 187)

What is characteristic in the whole scene with Geraldine is that, witnessing a dramatic exchange between the two girls, we receive what W. L. Myers calls "a definitely centred impression of personality"[1]: Geraldine is presented through Judith's impressions. Within minutes the shocked and hurt Judith sees Geraldine now as beautiful, now as repulsive and ugly (p. 140), and it is irrelevant and impossible to decide what she was "really" like: the fascination she exerts over Judith gains in persuasiveness through our heroine's ambivalent impressions.

The side or slanted view of most secondary characters (objects of observation of the narrator-agents) in Rosamond Lehmann's novels places the reader close to the consciousness of the central character (our centre of orientation). A recurrent preoccupation emerges: how far can one see the truth about people? This is the question asked by the three youthful heroines of Rosamond Lehmann in *Dusty Answer, Invitation to the Waltz*, and *The Ballad and the Source*, where the particular handling of the limited point of view of Judith, Olivia and Rebecca largely determines the presentation of the secondary characters. Among these one can distinguish two groups, which

---

[1] W. L. Myers, *The Later Realism: A Study in Characterization in the British Novel* (Chicago: Univ. of Chicago Press, 1927), p. 112.

W. J. Harvey calls the ficelles and the Cards.[2] The ficelle (as in Henry James) according to his definition, is

the character who while more fully delineated and individualized than any background character, exists in the novel primarily to serve some function. Unlike the protagonist he is ultimately a means to an end rather than an end in himself; the novelist's success in treating him will often reside in the function being so disguised that it may be performed unobtrusively.[3]

The Card, on the other hand, is "the character who is a 'character'."[4]

Despite the Card's difference from the protagonist, he too is an end-in-himself in the novel; any function he serves is a by-product. The danger of allowing a Card into a novel is that so exuberant is he in his autonomy . . . that he is liable to grow out of all proportion . . . The danger of the ficelle, on the other hand, is that he may seem merely a function, serving his purpose without the margin of gratuitous life which changes a schematic figure into an interesting character.[5]

In *Dusty Answer* the five cousins are "Cards", or ends-in-themselves, whom we view mostly in terms of their actions reported by Judith, but also through her impressions and conjectures, all mingled together, as in the following fragment:

Martin and Mariella came strolling back from the garden, the spark of their cigarettes going before them. She heard Mariella's little laugh bubbling out contentedly, her childish voice answering his in an easy chatter. Yes, Mariella was happy with Martin. He was polite and kind to her, and she was equal to him without effort. As she came into the light Judith was struck afresh by the lack of all emphasis, the careful absence of any memorable feature in the memorable whole of her beauty. Her [clothes] said "Mariella" and nothing else in the world. (p. 87)

The book opens with Judith remembering the cousins as children, and what they meant to her, each individually and as a group. She thinks of Mariella: "Apart from the thrill which her own queerness gave, she had upon her the reflected glory of the four boy-cousins" (p. 4). Judith does not so much think about what the children were like but rather what they meant to her and how it felt "to want to know and understand and absorb people to such a degree that it was a fever" (p. 5). Yet out of her early memories they emerge as very real, though only briefly sketched in a few sentences illustrated with short dramatic scenes (pp. 6—18). These show the children's essential characteristics—including Judith's—and the pattern of their relationships. Martin is devoted to Judith and Roddy, Roddy is Martin's best friend, Mariella—as Judith suspects—likes Julian best, Julian loves his beautiful and spoilt brother Charlie. Judith is least interested in Martin, Mariella intrigues her, she loves Charlie at first and then is fascinated by the withdrawn and

[2] W. J. Harvey, *Character and the Novel* (London: Chatto, 1965), p. 58.
[3] Ibid.
[4] Ibid.
[5] Ibid., pp. 62—63.

independent Roddy. Judith is interested in the unique quality of the cousins who, while remaining basically static throughout the novel, are sharply individualized. She thinks of a fundamental likeness between them (cf. above, p. 29), but in the context of the book they emerge as differentiated individuals. Against their scarcely changing characters Judith's own development is shown. But in the last portion of *Dusty Answer* her "degree of privilege"[6] is somewhat strained. It is achieved by a series of letters which explain by stating, not showing, the characters of Julian, Charlie, and, above all, Mariella. The letters round off neatly the leitmotif of Judith's childhood and adolescence: her infatuation with the group.

Other secondary characters belong to the background, like Judith's mother, or her college friend Mabel, and are not much more than types, though the latter is conveyed much more vividly: Judith takes for granted her mother's elegance and indifference, but she strongly reacts to Mabel's plaintiveness and physical repulsiveness. Thus the nature of Judith's sensibility conditions our access to all the secondary characters, and her feelings about them govern the amount of space they are given in the narration. Characters who are no more than ficelles appear rarely. There is, for instance, the old gardener Lacey, who brings to Judith the news of Charlie's death: by quoting his short account *verbatim* his character is intimated as the type of a devoted family servant: "We 'ad word from London this afternoon. Ah, it's cruel. It'll about kill his Grannie, that's wot I says first thing—about kill her it will" (p. 48).

The secondary characters in *Invitation to the Waltz*, except for Olivia's sister Kate and brother James (shown briefly from the inside) are all types who, against Olivia's presentation in depth, are characterized more fragmentarily. Most of the people Olivia meets at the ball appear only for a short instant, as she talks to or dances with them.

There is Lady Spencer, the majestic hostess:

She was always right. She knew it. (p. 155);

her husband Sir John, who greeted Olivia with

a look of mild benevolence [...] blent with a kind of gratified amusement, not unlike that which a mastiff assumes during the investigation of a puppy (p. 156);

the children of the house: Marigold,

freakish, vague, gallant and capricious (p. 158),

and Rollo,

---

[6] Booth, pp. 160—63.

superb in his pink coat, tall, ruddy, chestnut-haired, commanding, surrounded by his companions, every inch the only son of the house (p. 161);

two girls from the neighbourhood

Good old Martins. Where all was lost, their presence could always be counted on at the buffet (p. 180).

Among Olivia's dancing partners is Maurice:

He was a very rapid dancer. He danced on his toes and hopped like a grasshopper. This, combined with his hair and freckles, made him comically conspicuous [. . .] he made one think of some domestic fowl (p. 185);

Podge,

a heavy young man with a moustache and a bulging slow-motion grey eye (p. 217);

and an elderly gentleman

dancing with the youngest girls in the room one after the other; the girls drooping a little, pressed to his paunch. (p. 230) His skin was puckered and wrinkled, tortoise-like, under the chin, his cheeks puffy and veined with purple, his eyes a bit glazed and blood-shot. Otherwise he didn't look too bad. (p. 231)

There is an eccentric young poet who shocks Olivia, and a blind young man whose tragedy deeply moves her.

A whole gallery of people turn up in short scenes; everything is new and exciting to Olivia, who observes the world around her keenly, eager to note and learn as much as possible. Every one of these background characters is important and unique for Olivia, whose experience of people is still limited—this is the first time in her life she has met so many strangers, quite different from the people she has been used to from home. Ten years later, in *The Weather in the Streets*, she tells Rollo that at that dance she was seeing herself in "dozens of distorting mirrors" (p. 134) into which her own uncertainty and self-consciousness changed the others.

In *The Ballad and the Source* secondary characters are also presented through the eyes of a young and inexperienced girl, but here they combine the function of the Card—with his "margin of gratuitous life which changes a schematic figure into an interesting character"[7]—and the ficelle. In their function of ficelles they provide Rebecca with information about various fragments of Mrs. Jardine's life: this is their *raison d'être* in the novel. Let us examine one of them, Tilly, who is a marginal figure in the story itself, loosely associated with both Mrs. Jardine (by being her closest friend's maid) and with Rebecca, to whose home she comes as a seamstress. Thus she connects the past with the present, and her own very real presence imparts

[7] Harvey, p. 63.

60

life to the distant subject of her narration, even more so because she has a special interest in giving the child her own version of it, contradictory to Mrs. Jardine's interpretation.

Tilly is first mentioned at the beginning of the novel as an important person in Rebecca's early childhood. Her appearance and character are described in detail, so that when she reappears in Maisie's early memories as the missing link from the past, the reader recognizes Tilly at the same time as Rebecca. The precise and striking detail has a great identifying and suggestive power. Tilly

was a diminutive Cockney, just not a dwarf, cased always from head to foot in glossy black, with a little lace-bordered black silk apron, jet ornaments and a cornelian brooch. When she took the air, she wore a waist-length cape called a dolman, and a midget bonnet tied under the chin with broad black satin strings. Her reality belonged entirely to the Dickens world. She had a large pendulous face with caramel eyes on stalks, a long comedian's upper lip and chin, and on her bulging forehead a lump the size of a trush's egg, which she concealed by arranging over it one circular varnished curl [. . .] (p. 14)

Tilly combines the vivacity of the Card with the definite function of the ficelle: shortly after fulfilling her part she disappears for good from the novel.[8]

Upon meeting Tilly for the first time the reader learns that "she was a true Cockney, all sharpness, materialism, irony and repartee. She was also a consummate actress and mimic" (p. 14). These qualities are later displayed in her reminiscences, and in combination with her listener's reactions give a lively and comic touch to her account of Mrs. Jardine's romantic elopment from her first husband:

" 'E was the proudest feller—gentleman—I ever struck. She took and crushed 'is pride."
I saw the dual figure, the dove-girl-Mrs. Jardine, wrench something hard, like a seal or a charm, from the breast of a shadowy male figure, and crush it into fragments with the strong, short, ringed fingers I knew. [. . .]

---

[8] The characterization of Tilly's appearance bears a close resemblance to that of Mrs. Wix in *What Maisie Knew*:

> [Her hair] was dressed in a manner of which the poor lady appeared not yet to have recognized the supersession, with a glossy braid, like a large diadem, on top of the head, and behind, at the nape of the neck, a dingy rosette like a large button. She wore glasses which, in humble reference to a divergent obliquity of vision, she called her straighteners, and a little ugly snuff-coloured dress trimmed with satin bands in the form of scallops and glazed with antiquity . . . it reminded her pupil of the polished shell or corselet of a horrid beetle. (p. 27)

Both Mrs. Wix and Tilly have one painful memory, the first of her Clara Mathilda, the second of her Little Feller, both dead as young children, whose mention evokes similar reactions. Despite these similarities, however, their functions in the respective novels are different, since Mrs. Wix changes and grows to occupy a significant place in Maisie's life.

"How did she do that?"

"Oh, she tucked up 'er flouncy skirts and was off one summer's evenin'."

"I see," I said, untruthfully.

" 'E'd give a ring at the bell. 'Where is *Madame*?' 'E'd be all ready dressed up, you see, to take 'er to the opera or the ball. 'Oh, M*adame*? She went out some hours ago, Moossew. She left a note for you in 'er boodwar.' " Tilly minced, rolled her eyes stagily in the style of an imaginary French lady's maid. " 'Ah, thank you, Maree. You may go.' *'Oui, Moossew. Mercy, Moossew.'* Up the stairs 'e 'd walk, very slow and dignified—smellin' a rat, I wouldn't be surprised. There was the letter [. . .] Gone with the one I love. ... "

"Oh!" I gasped, fatally interrupting. "Is that what she really said?"

There was a dead pause; then Tilly said peevishly:

" 'Ow should I know? I wasn't there, lookin' over 'is shoulder, was I?" (pp. 65—66)

In Rebecca's description of Tilly there is a mixture of her impressions as a child together with occasional comments made from her perspective as an adult, which give an air of distance to Tilly, a specimen from an epoch long past. The same is true of another "Dickensian" character in *The Ballad and the Source,* Auntie Mack, who

was dressed in a black jacket and skirt, both of unusual length, fusty, dusty, thread-bare, trimmed with wide black braid and voluminously flared below the waist and knees. Her black blouse was secured at the throat by the largest cameo brooch I have ever seen; and in the addition she was hung with chains of various sizes and designs. Her narrow flat chest broadened to an abnormal convexity combined with meagerness in the hips [. . .] Desultory wisps hung round the expanse of her face and forehead like a tacked-on oddment of frayed and faded trimming. She had a flourishing sandy moustache and long pinkish-yellowish cheeks patched with freckles, bulging green eyes with white lashes, and a big solid yet somehow vacant assortment of features. She was just the type of figure—knocked about, unsuspicious, mildly monstrous—with whom a child is instinctively at ease: perhaps because it represents, for a child, some truth about the world. A clown's truth. I felt an instant affection for Auntie Mack. (p. 182)

Tilly and Auntie Mack exemplify Harvey's observation that "Card-like characters are, so to speak, chemically pure ... Their realism is one of intensity, singleness, vivacity; the realism of the protagonist is that of dilution, complexity and process."[9]

Rosamond Lehmann's talent for inventing vivid and expressive minor characters grasped in their essential quality, often comic and slightly caricatured—Harvey's "Cards"—is best manifested when they are seen through the fresh eyes of her young heroines. In *A Note in Music, The Weather in the Streets*, and *The Echoing Grove* secondary characters belong rather to the ficelle type and have a definite function in the general pattern of the novels. In *A Note in Music*, Clare is a female counterpart·of her brother and her role in the MacKays' life corresponds to that of Hugh's. The other

[9] Harvey, p. 62.

two characters, although presented from the inside, are fragmentary and dim: Christopher Seddon seems to be there solely for the plot's sake, and the poet Ralph (whose part in Hugh's story seems somewhat strained) is the author's mouthpiece, formulating the main theme of the novel (see below, p. 93).

Some of the secondary characters in *The Weather in the Streets* are more effective; for example Sir Ronald, Olivia's neighbour at the table at the Spencers' dinner party. Others, like Olivia's artistic friends, are supposed to possess certain qualities (Anna's integrity, Simon's spiritual power) of which we are only told by Olivia but which are shown unconvincingly or not at all: they are more a function of Olivia's interest in them than realized characters. There are also successful examples of impressionistic characterization of this kind, for instance the nurse at the end of the first part of the novel. She is seen through the prism of Olivia's particular mood, in this case a feeling of guilt and uneasiness at being probably suspected:

The blue eyes screwed down, cold, speculative, obscene. . . . Now what have *you* been up to? You're not the stand-offish sort, I know you. Come on now: no flies on me either, *Men*! [. . .]
Quick, quick, get away. . . .
"Well, good-night, nurse. Have you got everything you want?"
Ingratiating smile.
"Yes, thanks. Night-night."
The eyes stared, dropped, fastening quickly on the newspaper. . . . Baulked. (p. 141)

In *The Echoing Grove* the few secondary characters all have a definite function of contributing to the picture of the relationship explored in the novel. Thus Georgie, who becomes Rickie's mistress and confidante during the last days of his life, is to a large extent a variation or amplification of Dinah's character; Rob is to Dinah what Jocelyn is to Madeleine: a lover who disappoints her because his concept of conduct does not correspond to hers.

Whereas secondary characters are usually presented as the central awareness in the novel sees them, by means of description, relation, and interpretative commentary, the protagonists appear in action and through their interior monologues. The internal view is very important for characterization in those novels of Rosamond Lehmann in which the impact of external events on the character's mind is of central interest. This interiorization of characters has the power of winning sympathy for the protagonist, particularly when we see him or her alone, in adverse or inimical situations.

There is little information about the physical appearance of the protagonists, much less than in the case of many secondary characters. Their characterization is focused on the particular quality of their sensibility, which expresses itself in their perceptions, thoughts, and feelings evoked by definite

63

situations, presented from their point of view. Generally speaking, these mental processes can be recorded "either in the language of the author-reporter or in the very form and manner in which the moments of experience occurred ..."[10] In the latter case a character's own habits of thinking and even his vocabulary help to define his personality, for example Pansy in *A Note in Music*:

> There he was, there he was! Oh, what a jump her heart gave! ... Just as she had expected: she'd known he would be along some time. Lucky she had put on her black and white printed crêpe-de-chine, and her new hat. He was coming out of that Palace of Beauty ... And laughing fit to burst. He didn't look as if he'd admired them, anyway. No wonder. Beauty through the ages, indeed—Cleopatra, Helen of Troy, and all. Painted old tarts, she'd seen them. (p. 212)

Another consequence for characterization of presenting the world through the limited point of view is the fact that descriptions of nature take on a strongly subjective colouring. W. L. Myers observes that a particular mood or a characteristic manner in the description of a setting "becomes an emotional aura inseparable from the reader's recollection of a character and contributing largely to its power and sinigficance"[11] (see, for example, Grace in *A Note in Music:* p. 78).

A certain amount of direct characterization is sometimes provided by the author who, however, leaves it without any commentary of her own. Here belong the small physical gestures accompanying a character's conversation, as in *The Echoing Grove*, when Rickie, unable to solve his conflict with Dinah, is "sweeping bread-crumbs off the table into his hand and pouring them on to a plate" (p. 114)—a vicarious act of tidying up. Dinah interprets another of his characteristic gestures as significant: Rickie's trick of shutting his eyes:

> Had seen him do this a dozen, dozen times by the family hearth—never before with me. Had decided to my own satisfaction what it meant, in psychological terms: not tension, not active boredom—simply negativity. (p. 41)

The fact that not the author but another character in the book offers this comment gives it more actuality: it is shown as experienced in such and such a way within the book, and not as an external judgement.

These are, however, minor methods of characterization. Characters are primarily set forth in their interrelationships and, as W. J. Harvey points out, "it is ridiculous to isolate characters from a novel and discuss them as totally autonomous entities; the novel itself is nothing but a complicated structure of artificially formed contexts parallel to those within which we experience real people."[12] Apart from their interior monologues, characters are revealed

[10] Myers, p. 137.
[11] Ibid., p. 102.
[12] Harvey, p. 31.

in dramatic scenes. In *Dusty Answer* the two methods are combined, for even the major part of Judith's recollections, which occupy the first part of the book, is presented in dramatic form, either as actual conversations remembered by her, or as imaginary dialogues taking place in her dreams. The conversations and images in these dreams well dramatize her unformulated states of consciousness and epitomize her emotions and semiconscious drives. They are in keeping with Judith's character, for she is an intuitive and emotional personality who experiences the world primarily through feeling, not intellect. Her apprehensions about Charlie's life in wartime are shown in her dreams, sometimes reassuring, sometimes frightening (see pp. 41—47).

The very great importance of the human context for characterization has long been noted; Henry James maintained that "character, in any sense in which we can get at it, is action, and action is plot, and any plot ... plays upon our emotion, our suspense, by means of personal reference. We care for people only in proportion as we know what people are."[13] And again in "The Art of Fiction": "What is character but the determination of incident? What is incident but the illustration of character?"[14] Incident, which shows a character in his interplay with others, is by far the most prevalent method of characterization in *Invitation to the Waltz*. Every sub-chapter of the part devoted to the ball deals with Olivia's encounter with a new person, while in the first part of the novel each sub-chapter presents her in a different situation, all within the compass of one day. There is the birthday breakfast, at which Olivia is shown among her family. Next we see her at the dressmaker's, then on her walk home, meeting several people from the village, meditating on plants, death, and the declining health of her father. The rest of the day is typical, representative of many of Olivia's days: crying over *David Copperfield*, saying good-night to her little brother, playing ludo with her sister after supper. When we next see her outside her family, we know enough of her to give her our sympathy and look at the new scene with her eyes. Through the precise rendering of the impact of these small incidents on Olivia, her sensibility is firmly established. The particularity of the descriptions of the other secondary characters, each caught in his most salient feature, animates the whole scene and is representative of Olivia's way of looking at things.

In *The Ballad and the Source* the animating power of incident is replaced by the vitality of the characters who comment on Mrs. Jardine. The seemingly undramatic device of a story being told to Rebecca by several narrators is here skilfully used to develop them into vivid characters. Tilly,

---

[13] Henry James, "Anthony Trollope", in *Theory of Fiction: Henry James.* Ed. J. E. Miller, Jr. (Lincoln: Univ. of Nebraska, 1972), p. 200.
[14] Henry James, "The Art of Fiction", in *Selected Literary Criticism.* Ed. M. Shapira (Harmondsworth: Penguin, 1963), p. 88.

encouraged by Rebecca, tells her about Mrs. Jardine's youth, but a few days later the girl learns from Mrs. Jardine herself that Tilly deliberately left out an important chapter from her narration in which she herself was involved. This throws a new light on Tilly and her attitude to the main heroine.

Rebecca herself holds a special position in the novel, for she is our centre of orientation and therefore we get to know her most intimately. Yet her own life is left completely in the background and she is not an important participant in the story, which covers three generations and takes place in England, Italy, France, Scotland, and Bohemia. What is, however, of paramount importance in the book is Rebecca's perception of the story she hears. Her character is thus an integral part of the picture of Mrs. Jardine and affects it in much the same way that a specific point of observation determines an observer's range of vision. Rebecca's curiosity is aroused by Mrs. Jardine's note to her mother, asking her to let the children (Rebecca and her sister) come to tea with her. Mrs. Jardine writes:

"*We are getting too old to wander all our days, and Harry's torn roots in England and his childhood home have ached more and more with the passage of the years. ...*"

"Is that what she says?" I asked, startled. Immediately, I felt attracted towards a lady who expressed herself with such picturesqueness. (p. 5)

When Rebecca and her sister Jess call for the first time on Mrs. Jardine, they are impressed both by her looks and by her unconventional behaviour:

When she came up to us, she said:
"I must kiss you, because I loved your grandmother."
We lifted our faces, and she gave us each a kiss. Her lips and cheeks were dry, warm, the skin so crinkled all over with faint lines it seemed a fine-meshed net. The most noticeable things about her were the whiteness of her face, the paleness of her large eyes, and the strong fullness and width of her mouth. Her teeth were regular, untouched by age.
We were deeply struck by her remark. It sounded strange to us that a person should so reveal her feelings: we did not say things like that in our family, though I dreamed of a life in which such pregnant statements should lead on to drama and revelation. I had at this time a sense that I might be a more romantic figure than my parents and other people realized. (p. 10)

In this manner the character of Rebecca as a receptive and enthralled observer is established.

Although the novel is not concerned with Rebecca's fate, we see her gradual and convincing transformation from a child into an adolescent. The nature of Rebecca's interest changes, yet her curiosity is never finally satisfied, for Mrs. Jardine's character is far from being elucidated and explained: she remains opaque both to Rebecca and the reader. This fact contributes to the fascination of her character; W. J. Harvey seems to be right in saying that "it is a part of any character's mimetic adequacy that he should resist the encroaching lucidity of the reader".[15] An atmosphere of mystery pervades the climax of the story, recounted by Maisie to Rebecca, who listens with a "simple goggle-eyed expectancy" (p. 270). They find themselves in Mrs. Jardine's house on a Christmas night, while she is away in France. Yet everybody in the house is somehow aware of her presence and Rebecca

> could not get rid of a vision of her, high on the watch tower of a castle in France, directing upon us searchlight eyes over wastes of winter dark and ocean. Her glittering face blazed in the firmament, savage, distraught, unearthly: Enchantress Queen in an antique ballad of revenge. (p. 238)

Mrs. Jardine, like Miss Havisham in the eyes of Pip in *Great Expectations*, preserves this "spectral" quality to the very end.

Both protagonists and secondary figures in the novel are characterized by means of the most prominent element of dramatic scenes—dialogue. The vividness of dialogue is as a rule greater than that of direct methods of presentation, and its quality of presentness successfully creates an illusion of reality. In *The Ballad and the Source*, for example, the largest part of exposition, development, and conclusion is supplied in dialogue which enhances the sense of the actuality of Rebecca's relation, although we know that the conversations recorded took place long before Rebecca-the narrator recounts them. The principle of dramatization results sometimes in Chinese-boxes-constructions, as when Rebecca is listening to Tilly who re-enacts for her what Rebecca's grandmother told her what she in turn had been told by Mrs. Jardine, all in direct speech. These constructions reduce the time distance to a minimum and give the child an impression of actually witnessing the events.

In dialogue characters reveal themselves in their habitual forms of language and various mannerism and affectations—it has a self-revelatory aspect quite independent of what the characters may be saying consciously. Rosamond Lehmann uses it frequently for characterization, especially of minor figures, with great imitative skill and authenticity. We can easily hear many of her characters speak, for example Etty in *Invitation to the Waltz*:

> I just happened to meet Tony at a night club last week, and he said *wouldn't* I come down for their little shoot and a dance, and, my dear, it *absolutely* went out of my head *where* he lived and *who* his people were—you know my vagueness, darling—and as Podge was going down too, I simply *hopped* into his car yesterday and set off, and *next* thing I knew we were driving through a town and I said to Podge *where's* this and he said Tulverton—and then, my dear, of course I realized. (p. 168)

or Sir Ronald in *The Weather in the Streets*:

[15] Harvey, p. 71.

Vey've had veir cook close on twenty years here—did you know? I fink I must be acquainted wiv the whole of her extensive repertoire. She's a wonderful creature. Of course, she has her weak spots like all artists. But she has a way of doing veal [...] I shall reserve my forces for vat and enjoy vis course vicariously [...] I like to hear a lady admitting to a healthy appetite. From what I gavver, it's rare in vese degenerate days. (pp. 81—82)

Auntie Mack's speech (*The Ballad and the Source*) is equally idiosyncratic:

Love has not triumphed yet, but love will come. I tell Mrs. Jardine not to despairr. Maisie will rise on stepping stones—but it will be gradual. Maisie has been through deep waterrs. Oh, the pity of it all! [...] Poorr fellow!
    [...] I am much a sufferer from indigestion, a reeal martyrr. The Majorr's lavish boarrd has quite upset my stomach [...] I overindulged at tea. The sight of that dewy golden butter! —and all those fresh baked scones and dinky biscuits ... I *could not* refrain. Oh dearr, dearr me, I made a thorough pig of myself. I must suffer the consequences. (pp. 186—87)

Dialogue is not only indicative in the sphere of a character's language and speech. As J. Raban observes, "we expect characters to speak authentically, but we also expect their language ... to convey things about them which they could not phrase for themselves."[16] One may also add: the things that they *would* not phrase for themselves, as an egotistic undertone in Mrs. Jardine's account of her daughter's elopement with her former lover Paul, where apparently all her concern is for Ianthe:

Oh Paul! Ianthe! What could I do now for them but let them alone, permit them their own choice—to be lost to me, to ignore me, leave me in the outer darkness of lonely suspense and anxiety? (p. 155)

It is ironic that Mrs. Jardine, usually so perspicacious, is not aware of the full implications of her formulation. This one sentence demonstrates Rosamond Lehmann's ingenuity in characterization: she intimates a certain characteristic of Mrs. Jardine in a form both condensed and subtle.

2. Contrasting and Complementary Visions

The technique of the shifted point of view has important effects on characterization. Although characters are usually best revealed in their interpersonal contexts—in action and dialogue—the shifted point of view, by amplifying the reader's intrinsic knowledge of the characters, adds to his understanding of their motivation. This technique of the multiple point of view, aptly called

[16] Raban, p. 84.

"bouncing" by E. M. Forster,[1] is the organizing principle of *A Note in Music* and *The Echoing Grove*, while it has a subservient function in *Invitation to the Waltz* and *The Weather in the Streets*, which are predominantly the novels of one governing consciousness.

A Note in Music is based on the multiple point of view: dramatic events are for the most part told by the omniscient author who also introduces the reader into the minds of the characters. The narrative technique of this novel has been compared to that of Gide's and Huxley's in that "one person's experiences are set in contrapuntal relation to another's".[2] The conflicting inner visions offered in the book well illustrate its characters "whose lives are being lived at cross-purposes" and who are never able "to extricate themselves from false positions".[3] The bounced narrative is clearly ideal for a sympathetic presentation of several people's inner lives and for setting them impartially against one another. Because the point of view is shifted, there occurs no identification of the reader with the main characters, or at least it cannot last long, since we are soon "bounced" into another character's subjectivity. Therefore we view the characters from a certain distance which enables us to see a pattern in their relationships more clearly.

The characters—all except Grace Fairfax, with whom the novel opens—are first introduced through someone else's vision; for example, Tom and Hugh through Grace, Gerald through Norah, Pansy through Hugh. Then, having made themselves known to the reader by means of an interior monologue, they in turn introduce the next person through their personal view. This mode of the characters' existence, i.e. in another person's mind, is sometimes the only link between two characters who otherwise never meet and do not know anything about one another. Grace and Pansy are "related" only through Hugh and Tom. Still, there is a bond between them: their love for Hugh. And thus they both belong in the same orbit (we might say that Pansy stands in a somewhat similar relation to Grace as Septimus to Clarissa in *Mrs. Dalloway*) and both contribute to the establishing of Hugh's continuity in the novel: when he displays kindness to one of them and then, quite independently, to the other, this trait of his character is corroborated and convincingly dramatized.

The novel begins with Grace's interior monologue and her vision of subsequent events continues throughout Part I. In Parts II and III the point of view shifts from one person to another: Norah, Grace, Hugh, Norah again, Gerald, Tom, Pansy. Their inner monologues introduce the reader into their situation and their present moods and thoughts evoked in the course of action. The events of the plot are not only complemented by this kind of

[1] E. M. Forster, *Aspects of the Novel* (New York: Harcourt, 1954), p. 78.
[2] John Chamberlain, "Miss Lehmann's Second Novel, *A Note in Music*", *New York Herald Tribune Books*, October 30, 1932, p. 6.
[3] Ibid.

inner commentary—the two stand rather in the same proportion as the parts of an iceberg above and under water: it is obvious that the visible part is only a small segment of the whole. As an example we may take the scene when Grace, Norah and Hugh have tea together in Grace's house (pp. 44—50). Their conventional polite conversation is reported by the undramatized narrator. At the same time we get Norah's impression of Hugh: he reminds her of his sister Clare and of her youth, and it leads her to ask Hugh about Clare. Then she remembers that he is new in the town and may be lonely, and therefore kindly inquires about his social life. Suddenly, when Hugh jokingly implies that he prefers wine to tea, she remembers that wine was also her old lover Jimmy's favourite drink. Leaving, she cordially invites Hugh to visit her home. While Norah is making conversation, Grace observes Hugh intently. He seems to fill the room, she watches his features and finds them arresting. Then she remembers what her husband Tom said, that Hugh looked more like an artist—and she thinks it was stupid of Tom to apply a label like this. And when Hugh asks her abruptly if she minds his smoking a pipe, Grace—still having her husband in mind—replies quickly no, Tom always smokes a pipe. She imagines she can see a look of realization come into Hugh's eyes: he places her now as the wife of the red-faced fellow in the office of his uncle's company. She feels embarrassed, but all Hugh says is that Tom was very helpful to him on his arrival. We do not know what he is thinking, and the only inside view of him during the first part of the conversation is his disgusted recollection of his lodgings, called forth by Norah's question about his landlady. It provides information merely about his external situation, so that the first part of the meeting reveals Grace's romantic, and Norah's more practical, impressions of Hugh whose thoughts are hidden equally from them and from the reader.

Hugh stays on a few minutes longer after Norah's departure and waits for Grace to mend his torn hunting coat. Now it is his turn to observe her more closely. They exchange a few remarks which alternate with Hugh's impressions of Grace: he feels a slight curiosity about her and she embarrasses him—he feels as if detained despite himself by the things she does not say. When they finally part, Hugh brushes her away from his mind, while Grace is left musing about him, trying to imagine what his life is like. In the tea-party scene the impact of one character, Hugh, on the two women serves as a means of characterization. We see that Norah has a strong tendency to think with nostalgia and resignation about the past, while Grace, involuntarily comparing Hugh all the time with Tom, thinks about her husband with irritation.

The illusion of being "inside" a character is interrupted with every shift of the point of view. The fact that the reader is placed further away from the point of view prevailing a moment ago produces ironical effects, as when Grace fails to notice that Tom has hinted at his intimacy with a prostitute.

She is congratulating herself on how easily she can keep her own secret, that is her love for Hugh, and thinking that she would know if Tom had anything to conceal: "No doubt, men were more honest and transparent than women" (p. 298). Here her usual acuity has failed her and, as this is her strongest point, our sympathy withdraws a little, the emotional distance increases. What is gained here at the expense of closeness to Grace is the sense of the impossibility of communication between her and Tom, and, as this truth is driven home once more, the psychological realism of the scene is enhanced. This is a case of "dramatic irony [which] results from the reciprocal ignorance of the characters; they are opaque to each other as we are to each other in real life."[4]

Irony arises often from a juxtaposition of two characters' attitudes towards the same situation or phenomenon. Tom's ideas about his joining Grace in the country for his holiday,

saying good-day to rustics, supping off bread and cheese and beer, having a chat with a farmer, sitting on stiles—generally giving his attention, in fact, to rural conditions (p. 201),

acquire ironic overtones when contrasted with Grace's poetic and transported experience of the countryside. Tom is shown living on the trivial plane of existence. The limitations of his sensibility are grave handicaps within the framework of the novel's implied order of values, in which imagination ranks very high.

The interior monologues or reflections modify and amplify the external actions of the characters, and the shifted point of view, by enlarging the reader's perspective, is an additional factor instrumental in the delineation of human relationships. This technique reveals both the inner and the social self of a character, and the discrepancy between an inner comment and outer behaviour is in itself a method of characterization. Thus in *The Echoing Grove* the juxtaposition of several persons' experience of the same situation gains in intensity when the dialogue is accompanied by excursions into the minds of the characters. In one of the critical scenes between Rickie and Madeleine they are discussing, among other things, Dinah's conduct. The fact that Rickie cannot cease to feel responsible for Dinah is extremely painful to Madeleine who, however, is trying to evaluate her sister's behaviour objectively. Yet, reacting to certain things Rickie says, she cannot help feeling that

the tide was beginning to crawl in again: unpredictable tide that rose now and then from somewhere beyond the farthest point of ebb and swung them off the treacherous flats they stood on. She felt it start to lift her, stinging and cleansing the raw abscess in her breast. Hold on, she told herself, soon we shall be afloat, we shall have drawn one another in.

[4] Harvey, p. 71.

"I *have* seen her unsure of herself," she presently allowed. "It's when somebody whose opinion she values gives her a—real telling off. You didn't, I suppose?" (p. 87)

In *The Echoing Grove* the scenes of greatest emotional intensity are presented usually from one person's point of view, and they reappear later in another context in the mind of another person. In this manner new details and new emotional responses find their way into the narrative whose total effect depends on accumulation. The shifts of the point of view from one of the protagonists to another in *The Echoing Grove* affect the dynamics of the novel: the pattern of growth and development of the relationship between Rickie, Madeleine and Dinah is shown by means of scattered fragments which, when all the versions have complemented each other, make up a finished whole. The same holds true of the characters themselves, whose presentation from the inside in the monologues merges with additional information contained in the other persons' vision of them and in the dramatic scenes.

A repetition of the same scene or situation in the consciousness of two or more persons serves to characterize them more precisely by pointing out the differences of their responses and showing from the inside the importance they attach to a given question. Thus the characters are presented from different angles and there are no evaluative comments supplied by the author: this accounts for the fact that, as J. Raban pointed out, "in bounced narrative the reader has to make up his own mind about the characters."[5]

In the two other novels where the single point of view of Olivia Curtis is predominant—*Invitation to the Waltz* and *The Weather in the Streets*—contrast between the two sisters is a typical method of characterization (cf. above, p. 20). The sisters' contrasting behaviour in the same situation illuminates their characters and the opposition is naturally established. Kate functions as a foil to the protagonist. Olivia meets the world in innocence and full of expectations. Her naivety and absent-mindedness are contrasted with Kate's common sense and practicality, as in the following episode: when Olivia came back home from the dressmaker, she was told that a young person was waiting for her. Surprised, Olivia agreed to see her. It turned out to be a weak-looking girl with a suit-case, wanting to sell her lace work. Olivia, who was not in the least interested in lace, felt that it was the moment to say so, but somehow could not bring herself to say it bluntly. She tried hard to muster the courage to stop the interview, while the girl was showing her different pieces of lace and telling her about her paralysed mother. Out of pity Olivia spent all her money on an unwanted lace collar and afterwards, almost in tears, told Kate the whole story. Her sister immediately suspected what had never occurred to Olivia: that the collar was a cheap ready made one, and the girl's pathetic story invented (pp. 84—94).

[5] Raban, p. 36.

Psychological differences are presented more often in dramatic terms than through the shifting of the point of view from Olivia to Kate, which happens only sporadically. Olivia is too earnest and intense to afford a sense of detachment towards her own feelings. Nevertheless such a distance appears in the book whenever her experience is set against Kate's level-headed reactions. Thus in the scene of Olivia's dressing for the dance, to a certain extent we measure Olivia by Kate. Initially, Olivia is the centre of orientation, with the first and third person narration alternating. When Kate joins her, the centre of orientation is slightly shifted and we watch the exchange between the two sisters not exactly from Olivia's perspective. Yet the scene is interspersed with her perceptions shown from the inside and thus we view her with the sympathy and immediacy which usually accompany our internal knowledge of a fictional character:

Now for the dress.
After all, I shall probably enjoy the dance frightfully.
Quarter of an hour passed.
Kate put in her head round the door.
"Ready?"
Olivia was standing still, with leaden stillness, before the glass. [...] Uneven hem; armholes too tight; and the draping—when Olivia looked at the clumsy lumpish pointless draping a terrible boiling-up, a painful constriction from chest to forehead started to scorch and suffocate her.
"It simply doesn't fit anywhere. ... " The words burst from her chokingly. "It's the most ghastly—It's no good [...] I must simply *rip* it off and burn it and not go to the dance, that's all." She clutched wildly at the bodice, as if to wrench it from her.
Kate cried suddenly:
"You've got it on back to front!"
Olivia's hands dropped.
"Have I?" she said meekly.
"You would." With the asperity of relief Kate seized and reversed her hurriedly, plunged her once more through the armholes. (pp. 130—31)

All the time we do not lose sight of the comedy of the situation which is experienced as critical by Olivia herself. We might say that the point of view here is shifted not so much from one character to another, as that the distance towards the centre of orientation varies.

Both in *Invitation to the Waltz* and *The Weather in the Streets*, the shifts of the point of view from Olivia to other characters have, among other things, the function of giving solidity to her background. Moreover, we get an idea of how Olivia appears to her parents and sister. In the brief glimpses of their thoughts there is often contained the kind of information about Olivia that we could hardly gather from the point of view of Olivia herself. When she is quite confident that she has managed to conceal her love affair from everybody, we know through the short internal view of Kate's thoughts that she was mistaken:

Kate stole a look at her. Hollow-cheeked, inert. . . . A ghastly colour, greyish beneath the make-up. Thinner than ever. Blast her . . . and she'd been looking so much better, so happy: in love obviously: somebody with money it seemed like—those silk stockings, those expensive flowers [. . .] (p. 245)

By means of the shifted point of view Olivia is characterized as a member of her family: in particular her estrangement from her mother is set forth clearly. Even when the point of view is Olivia's, this alienation is visible in her interpretation of Mrs. Curtis' behaviour, as when Olivia happens to sit by her father's sick-bed when he wakes up from his serious illness. They talk, and then he drops off to sleep again. At this point Mrs. Curtis comes into the room:

His wife came in softly and stood by the bed. Barely perceptibly, her face altered, stiffened [. . .]
"Well . . . go and get ready for supper. I'll stay with him now."
I stole a march. I cheated. She should have had his first words, not I . . . I've betrayed her. . . .
Guiltily, under her mother's shuttered eyes, she disengaged their hands. (p. 56)

It is significant that Olivia is thinking about her mother at this point as "his wife". Olivia on the whole admires her mother but she feels there is a barrier between them. The truth of this is corroborated when we enter the mind of Mrs. Curtis who approves only of her other daughter, Kate:

Kate, bless her, had slipped with no trouble into a suitable marriage within easy motoring distance. [. . .] sitting over the fire nowadays, each with her knitting, they were very cosy, very happy together [. . .] The barrier between generations was dissolved [. . .] A comfort, yes, a comfort, now that Olivia . . . now that James . . . phases, we hope; phases, of course. (p. 57)

Both in *Invitation to the Waltz* and *The Weather in the Streets* the inside presentation of secondary personages is restricted (with few exceptions) to Olivia's home and those who stand very close to her. When she is outside her home, the centre of orientation is with her: she is a more or less detached observer of the social scene (the ball, the dinner party) and her isolation from the other characters is emphasized.

As we have seen, in *A Note in Music* characterization is based on the complementary inward views of several characters, and in *The Weather in the Streets* one of the methods of characterizing Olivia is the contrast between the two sisters. In *The Ballad and the Source* the ambiguous character of Mrs. Jardine is depicted through both complementary and contrasting visions of several characters presented on the exterior plane. The only interior vision is that of Rebecca, whose judgements are wholly intuitive and by no means imposed on the reader who is continually aware of her immaturity and lack of knowledge. *The Echoing Grove*, like *A Note in Music*, is a novel of multiple vision, where various subjective viewpoints are contrasted and the specific combinations of the limited points of view of

74

Rickie, Madeleine, Dinah, and others bear directly on the limitations of interpersonal communication. The shifted point of view is conducive to a dynamic, ever-qualified creation of character.

3. Repetition with Variation

The time element, so decisive for the establishing of the subjective vision of life, is of great consequence in the creation of character. Modern novelists have always been aware of the importance of the temporal aspect of a fictional character, and, judging by her novels, Rosamond Lehmann would surely agree with Ford and Conrad that in order to create a vivid character "you could not begin at his beginning and work his life chronologically to the end. You must first get him in with a strong impression, and then work backwards and forwards over his past."[1] This is indeed the way in which Rosamond Lehmann introduces her main characters in all her six novels. We have observed how the "inwardness" and interest in the subjective experience of the world (see above, p. 42) is reflected in the temporal structure of the novels and the selection of events described. There exists also a close relation between the time distance and the emotional distance between the characters (cf. above, p. 52—53). Furthermore, as we shall presently see, the passage of time as shown in the novels and the way it is experienced by the characters is of crucial importance in the drawing of their development.

In *Dusty Answer* we follow Judith in time from childhood through adolescence and the novel ends with her journey back home, the question of her future left open, the leitmotif of her childhood and adolescence exhausted. For the moment she feels happy, sure of herself, complete—in spite of the dusty answer to her ardent pursuit of certainties and her vehement urge to possess through understanding. She has grown up through her disillusionment to acknowledge her mistake, but she is still too close in time to the painful experiences to feel more than emptiness, "no-thought and no-feeling" (p. 355). The story of Judith's emotional progress from innocence to experience forms a *Bildungsroman* with a difference, for it has what Alan Friedman calls an "open ending",[2] in the sense that Judith's experience which underlies it is never closed: her progress is recorded with no final conclusion in view.

Judith's development is suggested both in terms of change from without and from within. The latter can be illustrated by her changed perception of the same things at different moments of time. Thus the college, which had

[1] Joseph Conrad, "A Personal Remembrance" (Boston, 1924). Quoted after Booth, p. 191.
[2] Alan Friedman, *The Turn of the Novel*, p. 15.

75

been an unfriendly and alien place at first, seemed quite the reverse on the eve of leaving:

The building, caressed with sunset, looked motherly and benign, spreading its sheltering breast for the last time above its midgets. New life might find nothing so secure and tranquil as its dispassionate protection. (p. 216)

When at the end of the novel Judith is going back home, she feels that her "whole past made one great circle, completed now and ready to be discarded" (p. 355), but even the home she is coming to is changed:

When she reached home she would find that the cherry-tree in the garden had been cut down. This morning she had seen the gardener start to lay the axe to its dying trunk. Even the cherry-tree would be gone. Next door the board would be up: For Sale. None of the children next door had been for her. (p. 355)

In *Invitation to the Waltz*, which covers only a very short period of time, Olivia's development is indicated in a different way: we see how she suddenly opens to new values, begins to question the things that she has always taken for granted and to look at them afresh:

[The three houses] were known in the family as Grandpapa's houses: for Grandpapa, the beneficient potentate, had built them [...] examples of modern improvement; and much local prestige attached to them. One must be very proud of all Grandpapa's works.... She looked at them. But surely—surely they didn't look very nice? ... in fact—horrid? Fancy Grandpapa having built such ugly houses. She summoned the portrait in the dining-room—the noble beard, the prosperous frock-coat, well-rounded waist-coat, all the marks of infallibility. She felt embarrassed [...] almost guilty. Fancy criticizing Grandpapa. (pp. 60—61)

Olivia's first dance is her initiation into the world of adults. When she goes out into the garden the following morning, she is already a different person, full of excitement about the future and looking with a certain distance at the familiar scene:

She hurried down the lawn, past the walnut tree, not stopping to swing, past the distant back view of Dad and Uncle Oswald taking their constitutional in the rose garden—two funny old brothers pacing together. (pp. 300—301)

In *The Weather in the Streets* Olivia often refers to the changes that have taken place during the ten years which have elapsed since the time of *Invitation to the Waltz*. Also within the course of the novel her attitudes towards past events become modified by new experiences. In fact the whole affair with Rollo is an experience in continual flux, whose different stages Olivia recalls in Part II of the book. In the beginning she congratulates herself on not being jealous of Rollo. But after a week-end spent together "things were different. I couldn't go back to those furtive snatched half-frustrated meetings" (p. 174). As time passes Olivia's love becomes more possessive. Once at a revue they saw a dancer:

She was enough to make any one hold their breath; I did, and I could feel Rollo spellbound. He didn't say a word afterwards, but clapped and clapped. I looked at him, smiling enthusiastically, and clapped too. But a terrible feeling came down to me . . . like sour thick carpet dust in my chest and windpipe. . . . The worst feeling of my life. (pp. 175—76)

The event belongs to a new stage of the affair, quite different from the untroubled initial phase.

The passage of time and the development and decline of the relationship is presented by means of the repetition of a situation with variation. In July Olivia and Rollo spent a day in the country with a group of her friends. They stayed in her friend Simon's cottage, decorated in the Bohemian style:

Simon's house is one to love, it's important, like a being with its own life and idiosyncrasies. It filled up a little of the emptiness [. . .] a channel for emotion. . . . Simon's house is poetic [. . .] It's by no means an architectural gem—yet it's entirely special. (p. 210)

Towards the end of the day they all went on to a pub:

The Wreath of May. Picturesque is the word for it—old, thatched, white-washed, sagging, full of beams. We sat outside on a bench against the front of the house [. . .] The light was rich and still, standing in simple gold shapes among the shadows. (pp. 218—19)

The evening was a great success. Then, at the end of September, Olivia and Rollo go back to Simon's house. Autumn has set in and, after an eventful summer, their love affair is turning sour. They feel they cannot stay in the house in which they were once so happy and, as they drive away, Olivia is thinking:

It was a small white house with green shutters and a leaded roof, set in a piece of neglected lawn: dismal, unwelcoming. Nothing special about it except the ragged torn hedge all round. The shrine was broken, the genius had departed. (pp. 319—20)

The Wreath of May turns out to be equally disappointing:

Now all was deserted. There was a ladder set up against the apple tree, three or four mongrel chickens pecking in the damp grass, a blue-painted, peeling garden table with a pool of wet on it [. . .] When she looked at the house, she noticed things she hadn't noticed before: only one wing was old, the rest was shoddy pseudo-old-war, with thin, poor thatching. (p. 320)

During the course of the evening the lovers quarrel violently and break up—summer and autumn in nature are paralleled in the world of the emotions. The time element plays inevitably against Olivia and she is aware of it throughout: "Naturally, relationships can't stand still, they must develop" (p. 215), she admits to herself resignedly.

In *The Echoing Grove* the presentation of the passage of time seems to lack a certain substantiation. The action of the novel covers some twenty years, but the characters, perhaps with the exception of Dinah, do not change deeply, apart from growing older. They lack some solidity since they seem to have no ordinary lives apart from the emotional crises which, devoid of a background, exist as if outside time.

The time dimension, however, is not equally important for the description of all the psychological phenomena in the books. Some perceptions take place, as it were, outside time. Some characters experience much of what is really significant in life as if in a flash, in one sudden moment of illumination. Such a moment of intense perception bestows a symbolic, universal meaning on otherwise disjointed sensations. These experiences, expressed by means of images, appear in all the novels of Rosamond Lehmann, although they do not occupy the focal position they have in the art of Virginia Woolf. We cannot exclude her influence here, and, as early as the publication of Rosamond Lehmann's second novel, a critic wrote that "it is to be suspected that Miss Lehmann has been reading Virginia Woolf and trying to emulate the older woman's skill at writing luminously of small things."[3] Whatever the influence might have been, in Rosamond Lehmann the method is put to a different use since her characters do not perceive the world predominantly in such flashes of vision.

The moment of illumination in which one suddenly realizes a deeper meaning underlying our experience appears as early as *Dusty Answer*, where it comes to Judith after she has learned about the death of her father:

> There was nobody in the garden. A faint light was abroad—it might be the small rising moon or the dawn—making the cherry-tree pale and clear. It seemed to float towards her, to swell and tower into the sky, a shining vision.
> Then death, lovely death, lay at the heart of enchantment. It was the core of the mystery and beauty. To-morrow she would not know it, but to-night no knowledge was surer. And he whom they were to mourn was—in one minute she would know where he was—one minute.
> She leaned out the window.
> Now! Now!
> But the cherry-tree was nothing but a small flowering cherry-tree. Before her straining eyes it had veiled itself and withheld the sign. (p. 120)

In *A Note in Music* it is Grace whose vision of the world is based on such illuminations. For example, lying once on a beach, she looks at the evening sky and a lonely child with a shrimping-net, and suddenly

> all had become fixed, crystallized into forms absolute and eternal. Earth and sky mirrored each other in a blue element half air, half water, the lonely child bent for ever above her net, the breaking wave spread itself at the edge of the unmoving fields of the sea like a long bank of flowering marguerite daisies. (p. 38)

It is a moment of self-forgetfulness and pure contemplation of perfection.

[3] Chamberlain, p. 4.

The function of these moments of illumination has been observed by J. W. Harvey who writes:

One of the distinguishing features of much modern fiction is its concern with epiphany, the Wordsworthian "spot of time," the moment of intense vision which yields significance far beyond the mundane world of common experiences ... it will ... have implications for the creation of character; to put it at its crudest, some characters will be capable of the moments of vision, others not. This capability is indeed often made the basis of moral judgement and discrimination.[4]

It is an index to value in the characters of *A Note in Music,* or at least this capability is considered a value in itself, pointing to an extension of sensibility. An experience of timelessness in the characters' otherwise temporal existence brings them nearer a certain intuitive truth about life.

Although the moments of vision are a rare and uncommon experience, it is impossible to view them as an individualizing trait in characters: one semi-mystical experience of this kind reads very much like another. It is rather a repetition of behaviour, a certain predictability and consistency underlying a character's development in time, that enables the reader to recognize the typical features of a person which differentiate him from all others.

In *The Ballad and the Source* a repetitive pattern of behaviour serves to describe a family in which some characteristic qualities reverberate for three generations. Such repetitions intensify some traits and give unity both to the family as such and to the structure of the book. Repetitions, however, occur with variations, and we can observe both similarities and differences between the members of the family as a unit and in their individual development. Mrs. Jardine loses her daughter Ianthe and later, though in a different way, she fails to keep her grandchildren. She tries to steal her own daughter from her husband, as later Ianthe tries to get her dead daughter Cherry back. Ianthe, like her mother, writes a novel about her life. Gil says about Mrs. Jardine what she has said about Ianthe: that they have built themselves a room of mirrors out of other people instead of looking directly out to the world. When Auntie Mack tells Rebecca about Maisie's independence and stubbornness, it resembles Tilly's pronouncements about the young Miss Sibyl (Mrs. Jardine). Rebecca is not unaware of this continuity, yet she senses a decline in the grandchildren from the grandeur of Mrs. Jardine: a decline which is paralleled in her own feeling of identity as compared to the magnificence of the past:

Portraits, letters, albums in the library, family legends, all conspired to float these grandparents, dead before our birth, glamorously before us. Figures larger than life size surrounded them, mingled with them in a rich element of culture and prosperity. In that lost land it was always midsummer; and the handsome, the talented, the

---

[4] Harvey, p. 64.

bearded great moved with Olympian words and gestures against a background of marble-columned studios, hallowed giant writing-desks, du Maurier-like musical drawing-rooms, dinner tables prodigious with good fare, branched candlesticks and wit. (pp. 12—13)

When Mrs. Jardine appears in Rebecca's life, she is a part of this past, which in Rebecca's eyes endows her with additional splendour. Mrs. Jardine lives up to the child's expectations and acquires an almost mythical stature. Ianthe, whom Rebecca never meets directly, is steeped in mystery, but Ianthe's daughter Maisie grows up to be all but a glamorous woman:

Her figure, considered as a woman's figure, was disastrous: heavily square in the shoulders, thick waisted, her bosom a solid plateau, aggressive yet uncompromising, the lower half of her squat and study, with muscular thighs and calves like a footballer's.

Not a line, not a feature recalled her grandmother; but all the same, each time I looked at her, a baffling echo of Mrs. Jardine brushed my senses [...] It was Maisie's stance, feet planted, head thrown back on the short neck? ... It was the way she sat herself down, back erect, knees a little spread? ... or the thing her eyes did, fixing and dilating? Or the incisive edge she put upon her last remark? (pp. 225—26)

This likeness shared by a group of characters reciprocally illuminates them, and we come to see certain qualities at the core of their being as essential and real.

In *The Echoing Grove* Rickie recognizes a basic similarity between the two sisters, Dinah and Madeleine:

"She's very resilient."[says Madeleine about Dinah]

He was moved to remark aloud upon the similarity of the comments these girls made about one another; he refrained. (p. 121)

He fell asleep at once and dreamed that he was bouncing two hard rubber balls on the asphalt floor of something like a school games yard [...] Bounce, bounce, higher, higher! "Look out!" "It's quite all right," said he, or someone, reassuringly. "They're made of elastic. Very, very, very resilient."

The floor began to crack and tilt. (pp. 123—24)

Another factor throwing light on the characters is the use of recurrent images and symbols. They are employed consciously and deliberately in the books of Rosamond Lehmann; as J. Raban observes, "the contemporary writer occupies rather a special position; he is likely to be ... familiar with the assumptions of psychoanalysis which have considerably influenced our ideas of the importance of symbolism."[5] The characters of Rosamond Lehmann are also as a rule conscious of a symbolic meaning of things, but this (that is, the fact that the symbols are thus often "explained"), does not, in my opinion, detract from their enriching function in the novels.

In Rosamond Lehmann's novels the background often has an imaginative relevance to the characters' situation or mood. In *A Note in Music* there is an

[5] Raban, p. 103.

image of a poor lilac tree in front of Grace's house which illustrates the transformations she undergoes during the spring and summer of Hugh's stay in the town. Coming back home after their chance meeting in the park, Grace saw that "suddenly the lilac tree was in full leaf, and there, at the top, were two or three clusters of whitish buds. It was years since it had flowered" (pp. 93—94). And when Hugh sees her home after their picnic in the country, she sees in the lilac tree a symbol of her own flowering:

Like her lilac tree, she thought, looking at the few white blooms which to-day's sun had unfolded fully, she was to be re-created after many years. She reached up and picked a head.
  "White lilac," she said. "I'm very proud of my tree. Do you like the smell?"
  She wanted so much to give it him. . . . She held it out awkwardly.
  "Thanks awfully," he said. "I love a button-hole. [. . .]" (p. 178)

Similarly, the cherry-tree in *Dusty Answer* has been associated with Judith throughout the novel. It has a special significance for her, and at one point she says: "Cherry blossom grows from the seeds of enchantment" (p. 114). The cutting down of the tree symbolizes the end of the phase in her life where enchantment was at the core of her experience. The recurrent images of the lilac and the cherry-tree have a binding function in the two novels' structures.

Parallels between the mood or behaviour of the characters and some quality of the external world appear both in *A Note in Music* and in *The Weather in the Streets*: an example of this might be the use of the weather as a tone-setting factor. As Norah hurries home after her visit to Pansy, "Another storm was piling in the tormented west, spreading across the sky. The gale was growing wilder. It would howl all night through" (p. 272). At home there awaits her a dramatic confrontation with Gerald, the first major crisis in their marriage. After the stormy scene Gerald comes up to her room, they quietly talk the situation over and are finally reconciled.

The worm ceased from its agitation. He was not thinking about Clare's beauty any more.
  "The gale's died down," she said. "Thank goodness, David won't get religion to-night. Look at the moonlight on these roofs! What a lovely night!"
  [. . .] And he sat on in silence beside her; thinking that [. . .] if the final relinquishing of all that one had wanted could continue to be so graceful, so simple and serene as now it seemed; if one could go on holding one's wife's hand in peace and weariness, and never be made jealous, never be enraged by her any more—then age might lose its sting, the grave its victory. (pp. 292—93)

In *The Weather in the Streets* there is a similar correlation between the weather and the mood of Olivia. The book opens with Olivia's favourite mild weather:

The sky's amorphous material began to quilt, then to split, to shred away; here and there a ghost of blue breathed in the vaporous upper rifts, and the air stood flushed with a luminous essence, a sort of indirect suffusion from the yet undeclared sun. It would be fine. My favourite weather. (p. 10)

The weather proves to be a good omen, for on that morning she meets Rollo. Their first week-end together begins with the same mild weather that Olivia likes. When some months later she is unhappy and in trouble, alone in London's summer heat, Lady Spencer's long dreaded visit comes on such a day:

A bad afternoon. The park was airless. The sky was clouding from the west, saffron-tinged: the fine spell would have broken before night. There would be thunder and then the rain would come down. She was restless, waiting for a change, unable to breathe. (p. 271)

Their conversation, most painful to Olivia, is accompanied by a storm: "The room had grown suddenly dark. Outside a thunder-shower broke sharply, rattling on the pavement" (p. 277). And a few minutes later:

"[...] Has something happened I don't know about?" Rollo, where are you? How could you? ... Tortured, and you don't care. ...
Lady Spencer was silent. Outside the rain redoubled for a moment, then suddenly sighed itself out.
"Rollo is weak," continued the voice implacably. (p. 278)

The scene ends on a quieter note. When Lady Spencer leaves, the rain is over and, as they both remark (p. 283), the air is fresher.

Another instance of this correlation between the natural and the emotional worlds is the lovers' last weekend together—a failure marking the end of their relationship. "The weather was dull, gusty, with clouds and wind coming up" (p. 314), "A peevish weather, hostile to man" (p. 317). They quarrel and Olivia runs out into the night:

How dark, I can't find the road; the wind, what a wind, a gale, I hadn't noticed; the wind from the Atlantic, the equinoctial gale. When it died down for a moment a sound came after it like giant tumbrils rolling and snarling in caverns in the sky. (p. 337)

Thus it is clear that "stormy weather is equated with Olivia's unhappiness, mild weather with happiness"—as Diana LeStourgeon writes.[6] She also rightly emphasizes the symbolical character of the "weather" of the novel's title: the weather is suggestive of Olivia's emotions. Being with Rollo meant safety and comfort, both physical and spiritual:

Beyond the glass casing I was in, was the weather, were the winter streets in rain, wind, fog, in the fine frosty days and nights, the mild, damp, grey ones. Pictures of London winter the other side of the glass—not reaching the body; no wet ankles, muddy stockings, blown hair, cold-aching cheeks, fog-smarting eyes, throat, nose ... (p. 145)

[6] LeStourgeon, p. 78.

The juxtaposition of the reality outside "the glass casing", in which Olivia normally lives, and the sheltered privileged life of Rollo is also expressed by means of the weather imagery:

There was a cold wind blowing, I shivered. There it was, Rollo's house [. . .] Lights in a room on the right of the door, the curtains parted a bit so that I could see in, and I saw him [. . .] From outside the room looked warm, rich and snug—a first-class comfortable home. (pp. 183—84)

The weather motif in this novel may be called, after E. K. Brown,[7] an "expanding symbol". It economically evokes Olivia's emotional situation and the two elements mutually enrich each other, the meaning "expands" as they change, in contrast to "fixed" symbols in which there is "no complication, subtilization, or expansion of meaning".[8]

Another example of an expanding symbol is the rabbit in *Dusty Answer*. In the beginning of the novel, when one of the children incidentally kills a rabbit with a stone, the realization of death comes as a great shock to Judith. Roddy, trying to comfort her, helps her to bury the rabbit, and since then the image of a dead rabbit remains for Judith associated with him. When years later she is a witness of Martin's shooting a rabbit, she immediately recalls the former occasion and re-lives, equally upset, the cruelty of an innocent animal's death:

She knew how it was looking—laid on its flat side and showing the tender and vulnerable whiteness beneath the frail still paws. [Martin] was stooping just as a figure had stooped above that other rabbit. . . . What years ago! . . . Roddy's rabbit whose death and burial had started this awful loving. Who was it devilish enough to prepare these deliberate traps for memory, these malicious repetitions and agonising contrasts? (p. 275)

But the first time she was reconciled to the rabbit's death: when they had buried it, it was

no longer terrible and pathetic, but dignified with its memorial tablet, lapped in the kind protecting earth, out of reach of flies and boys and the mocking stare of the sun. It was all right. There was not any sorrow. (p. 25)

Now it is all different: Judith collapses and cries hysterically because this time, after her failure with Roddy, she identifies herself with the rabbit:

Oh, the world! . . . No hope, no meaning in it; nothing but perversities, cruelties indulged in for sport, licking of lips over helpless victims. Men treated each other just as Martin treated small animals. (p. 275)

That night she has a dream about Roddy and the rabbit, which illustrates her disappointment in him. In the dream they sat "on the hill, close to where the

---

[7] E. K. Brown, *Rhythm in the Novel* (Toronto: Univ. of Toronto Press, 1950), pp. 32—59.
[8] Ibid., p. 42.

rabbit had been shot, and conversed in friendly fashion" (p. 278). Roddy talked about his mistresses, indifferent to Judith:

> It seemed then there was no use in hoping to win him back. He was, obviously, bored to death with her.
> "What's in here?" he said suddenly, and plunged his hand into the earth.
> The rabbit! ... The rabbit! ... Everything shrieked—and she started awake, sweating, in horror and desolation. (p. 279)

The symbol of the rabbit grows "as it accretes meaning from a succession of contexts".[9]

All the elements touched upon here—the passage of time as experienced by the characters, moments of illumination, repetitive patterns of behaviour, recurrent images, the expanding symbol—contribute to the drawing of characters. The time factor forms the basis of these methods of depicting characters whom we see dynamically, in development, through "repetition with variation".

[9] Ibid., p. 9.

Chapter IV

The Sphere of Human Relations

In Chapters II and III we have seen how the novels of Rosamond Lehmann are organized and the characters drawn within the subjective vision of life. Now it is time to examine how the subjective vision of life is reflected in the quality of human relationships presented in the novels.

It is my conviction that the picture of human relations is inseparable from the artistic techniques discussed in the previous chapters. This view naturally presupposes what René Wellek calls "the inseparability and reciprocity of form and content" which is almost universally accepted today.[1] " 'Form' ", say W. K. Wimsatt and Cleanth Brooks, "in fact embraces and penetrates 'message' in a way that constitutes a deeper and more substantial meaning than either abstract message or separable ornament."[2] And so the subjective vision in Rosamond Lehmann belongs both to her way of expression and the content of the books. It is therefore not accidental that the technique of the limited point of view should be applied to an examination of the limitations of interpersonal communication, individual experience of reality and illusion (Section 1), and the problem of personal isolation (Section 2).

In Section 3, "Fragmentation of Life", the novels are examined from a more general perspective, against a broader background and concerns shared by most modern novelists. This discussion aims at showing to what extent the fiction of Rosamond Lehmann is representative of its time.

1. Reality and Illusion

Rosamond Lehmann seeks to present a personal sense of reality as experienced by her characters. This is a widespread tendency in the literature of our period, the time of the questioning of many long and generally accepted values. The result is that both in life and in literature "the personal sense of truth replaces the formulas of a civilization."[1] When truth becomes a matter of individual perception and judgement, the problem of reality and

[1] R. Wellek, *Concepts of Criticism* (New Haven and London: Yale Univ. Press, 1973), p. 55.
[2] W. K. Wimsatt and Cleanth Brooks, *Literary Criticism* (New York: Routledge, 1957), p. 748.
[1] Daiches, p. 78.

illusion becomes particularly acute. What a character experiences as reality shapes in turn his or her interpersonal relations.

In the thoughts of Rosamond Lehmann's young heroines, "dream" and "mystery" are often recurring words. In *Invitation to the Waltz*, for example, Olivia once saw with surprise that her own face in the mirror "was a mysterious face" (p. 12), whose expression spelled change. Since that occasion she had been waiting in vain for a dramatic turn in her life, a revelation that she expected would rend the "veils of illusion [which] seemed to float over the familiar scene, half-hiding, half-revealing it under an eternal aspect" (p. 62).

The ball is Olivia's first step towards the revelation of a new reality. But at first the new experiences at the dance come to her as if in a dream. "The dream was beginning to deepen" (p. 225) when her attractive older cousin Etty from London chatters with her as with an equal, or when one of the boys behaves arrogantly and she does not understand why: "The dream was at its darkest, most irresponsible, most threatening" (p. 265). But when later in the evening Rollo, the splendid son of the house, takes Olivia to his father's library, she feels that this is what real life is like:

They [Rollo and his father] were so kind. This was what real people were like after all [...] not sinister, inexplicable, but [...] accepting one pleasantly, with humour but without malice [...] How extraordinary to be here with them; from being outcast, flung beyond the furthest rim, to have penetrated suddenly to the innermost core of the house, to be in their home. The dancing, the people beyond were nothing, a froth on the surface, soon to be blown away. (p. 280)

Olivia is shown standing on the threshold of the grown-up world. We see her horizons expand and her excitement grow at the opening of new vistas. The veils of shadow (illusion, ignorance) are being dispersed in the final scene of the novel, symbolizing her leap into a new future reality:

She leapt across a mound. Everything's going to begin [...] All the landscape as far as the horizon seemed to begin to move. Wind was chasing cloud, and sun flew behind them. A winged gigantic runner with a torch was running from a great distance to meet her, swooping over the low hills, skimming from them veil after veil of shadow, touching them to instant ethereal shapes of light [...] In a moment it would be everywhere. Here it was. She ran into it. (pp. 301–302)

The leap into the adult world has proved disappointing for Olivia whom we meet again in *The Weather in the Streets* ten years later. In the meantime she had gone to college, married a young poet and, after having lived with him for a few years in poverty, decided that they married too young and separated. She has lived alone for a year in London, with her cousin Etty, and when the novel begins, her half-hearted attempts at writing and helping a painter friend to run a photographer's studio are her chief occupations. She stills displays the same sensitivity to nature, is perceptive and open to new experiences, but in her relation with people has grown more cautious and discerning. This is a defence she puts up against the world, but Rollo remembers and recognizes the "dreamy" quality in her which singled her out as an adolescent and which attracts him now. Olivia's present life is cheerless and dull:

the book taken up, the book laid down, aghast, because of the traffic's sadness, which was time, lamenting and pouring away down all the streets for ever; because of the lives passing up and down outside with steps and voices of futile and forlorn commotion: draining out my life, out of the window, in their echoing wake, leaving me dry, stranded, sterile, bound solitary to the room's minute respectability, the gasfire, the cigarette, the awaited bell, the gramphone's idiot companionship, the unyielding arm-chair, the narrow bed, the hot-water bottles I must fill, the sleep I must sleep. . . . (p. 77)

Olivia meets Rollo on a train home and with his appearance a part of her early youth comes back to her mind. She tells him how romantic she used to feel about his whole family:

you were fairly drenched in glamour. Especially you [. . .] You flotated in a rosy veil. Marigold [Rollo's sister] was always feeding us up with accounts of you, and everything you did sounded so superior and exciting. You didn't seem real at all—just a beautiful dream. Of course it was a very long time ago. (p. 15)

But in fact she still feels very much the same about the Spencers and when her affair with Rollo begins, the old feeling gives it a dreamlike flavour. When Rollo sees her home after a dinner party, they kiss and she agrees to meet him in London. Coming into her house she is thinking: "This is with whom it was to be, and this is the night. Now I am back at the beginning, now begins what I dreamed was to be" (p. 136). Her father's nurse meets Olivia in the passage upstairs and she is forced to talk to her for a while, most unwillingly, for she does not want anybody to disrupt her mood:

Oh, stop, awful voices, glib voices rubbing, rattling against each other [. . .] Is it true, can it be true, what was said, felt, half an hour ago? Are the shapes still there, perfect as we left them, in the November night [. . .] Is the night still beautiful as it seemed—penetrated with moon, with warm leaf smell, cold smell of mist, secretly dying and living? Is it all nothing? Can it be defaced, deformed, made squalid by a voice? Could it be seen in some other way—in her way, not mine? (p. 140)

When Rollo told her at the dinner that he had wanted to see her again ever since they met ten years ago at Marigold's going out dance, "it sounded preposterous—like a voice in a dream" (p. 90). Falling in love seems a dream, beautiful and hard to believe. But once it happened, the plane of everyday existence seems unreal and insignificant. The reality of love supplants the world of facts, all the more so because the scene of their love is removed from Olivia's everyday life:

it was mostly in the safe dark, or in half-light in the deepest corner of the restaurant, as out of sight as possible. Drawn curtains, shaded lamp, or only the fire. (p. 145)

Their affair has to be clandestine, and only afterwards does Olivia see

what an odd duality it gave to life; being in love with Rollo was all-important, the
times with him the only reality; yet in another way they had no existence in reality
[...] Our lives were occupied, arranged without each other; the actual being together
had to be fitted in. (p. 161)

And yet Olivia comes to concentrate exclusively on her love for Rollo,
particularly since she has no other strong ties or commitments in her life.
When she feels for the first time that their relationship is threatened, she acts
as if her being together with Rollo were the only normal condition of her life.
This feeling comes shortly after she has been to his house, and they are
together on one of their weekend escapades out of London. At night Olivia
cannot fall asleep, being tired and on edge. She starts crying and Rollo
wakes up, horrified, but she finds it difficult to explain to him what is the
matter. The fact is that she is jealous of his wife, Nicola, for the visit to their
home—in Nicola's absence—makes her aware of the reality of Rollo's family
ties. But he manages to comfort her, and after a while "Life turned itself
inside out again, like after a bad dream, showing its accustomed unsinister
face. I thought I'd been mad. What on earth was the fuss?" (p. 195).

Because the whole experience is presented only from Olivia's point of view,
one might ask how adequate was her evaluation of the actual situation
between the lovers. Her final disappointment and the disintegration of her
relationship with Rollo are due not only to the hostile world of social
convention. When she visits him for the last time, she suddenly perceives
Rollo in a new light, and with an unpleasant feeling of unreality, for she
cannot believe that what for her was of essential importance, for him is fit to
be talked about in a facile and contented tone:

"I wanted terrible to ring you up and ask you [...] Only I didn't know if you were
still angry with me." He lowered his voice, coaxing, plaintive.
A feeling of unreality began to float her away. Really, the things he said! [...]
Oh, give it up, what's the use, we don't understand one another.... The unreality
was encroaching everywhere, blurring every outline. She was conscious now of
nothing but him sitting there, bulking so large, almost touching her [...] (pp.
380–81)

His manner, however, conforms now with the Rollo we meet earlier who
does not like complications and is all for an easy life. He used to warn
Olivia against taking him too seriously and expecting too much of him, "as if
he wanted to dismiss himself, shrug off the responsibility of being himself" (p.
167), thinks Olivia. "I hate gloom [he tells her]. For myself or any one else.
It's so uncomfortable" (p. 66), and when she wonders if he minds practising
deceit on his wife, he denies it: "What people don't know about can't hurt
them, can it?" (p. 160). Thus Olivia with a part of herself has known all the
time the real character of her lover, but chose not to dwell on his weaknesses,
for the state of being in love brought to her life a new happiness and

purpose. A rational understanding of Rollo, however, does not make the inevitable end of the affair any easier for her emotionally. Giving him up means not only the loss of a lover: it means going back to a lonely and empty life, where "individual relationships and other people's copulations and clothes and motor-cars" (p. 182) stand in the centre of one's interest.

The waking up from the happy interlude with Rollo is like passing from one unreality to another, for the empty life to which she returns is not real either, in the sense that it does not touch upon her innermost potentialities—hers is a frustrated life. She is not the only character who suffers in this way, for even the once admired and glamorous Marigold, who apparently has all the chances for self-realization, has a sense of futility even stronger than Olivia's. She admits to her former friend that she often feels as if she were not real: "It's a beastly feeling. Everybody has a solid real life except oneself. One's a sort of fraud ... empty" (p. 101). This sense of futility, unfulfilment and unreality pervading the world of *The Weather in the Streets* may be said to reflect a more general contemporary social climate (cf. Chapter IV, Section 3 below).

Olivia's experience in *Invitation to the Waltz* is similar to the young Judith's perception of the world in *Dusty Answer*: both are permeated with a sense of mystery and enchantement. In the happiest moments of Judith's early childhood, nature and human faces are full of promise:

It was autumn [...] All the blurred heavy garden was as still as glass, bowed down, folded up into itself, deaf, dumb and blind with secrets [...] When the children came from hiding in the bushes they looked all damp and tender [...] They were beautiful and mysterious like the evening. (p. 8)

The theme of *Dusty Answer* is Judith's romantic disillusionment and a gradual loss of the sense of mystery and hope which characterizes her at the beginning of the book. At the end she writes to Julian: "Enchantment has vanished from the world. Perhaps it will never come back, only in memory" (p. 235). Judith's development is shown in terms of the illusion-reality opposition. At first she is a lonely and imaginative child whose sheltered life furthers her tendency to day-dreaming and the concentration of her feelings on the group of older children next door. As a little girl Judith dreams about the most beautiful of them, Charlie, and her fantasies form an important part of her inner reality, although she can see clearly that her fascination is not returned. She dreams that

she fell ill herself, worn out with watching and anxiety [over Charlie]. Charlie came to her and with tears implored her to live that he might show his gratitude. Sometimes she did; but sometimes she died; and Charlie dedicated his ruined life to her, tending her grave and weeping daily [...]

Nothing in the least like that ever really happened in spite of prayers. He was quite indifferent. (pp. 10—11)

After Charlies's premature death in the war, Judith's infatuation is transferred to Roddy. In childhood "Roddy was the queerest little boy. He was the most unreal and thrilling of all because he was there so rarely" (p. 18). He was also the most withdrawn of the five children and "there was a suggestion about him of secret animals that go about by night" (p. 19). When he reappears in Judith's life as a young man, she is ready to love him and feels that it is going to be a love story with a happy ending. The reappearance of the whole group is a long-awaited and potent experience. The sudden realization that they have really returned comes to Judith almost as a shock:

Half-way back to the house she stopped suddenly, overcome with bewilderment; for that had been Roddy's self, not his shadow made by the imagination. The solitudes of the darkness now held their very forms, were mysterious with their voices where for so long only imagined shapes had hovered in the emptiness. . . . They had slipped back in that lucid, credulous life between waking and sleep out of which you start to ponder whether the dream was after all reality—or whether reality is nothing but a dream. (p. 57)

During their meetings that summer Roddy does not reveal himself much and Judith goes on loving him, or rather her own image of him, looking in vain for clues in Roddy's behaviour to any commitment on his part. Thoughts of him are constantly with Judith, for instance: "The evening held Roddy clasped within its beauty and mystery: he was identified with its secret" (p. 90). Mystery and romance as felt by Judith are genuine enough, but the object of her love remains elusive and time and again we see how she clings to her illusion of Roddy and refuses to accept him as he is:

"You're what I choose to think you are. There's no point in heaping yourself with abuse. You can't make me dislike you; you can only make me sad" (p. 169),

says Judith when Roddy tells her plainly that her hopes in him are unfounded. Therefore, when the inevitable disappointment comes, she has only herself to blame for her own stubbornness in adhering to the illusion of her own making. Her whole world collapses but she is honest enough to acknowledge her mistake and get to the root of it. This is a major step in her growing up. As she sees Roddy through a window of a teashop, talking to his friend in the street, she is thinking:

What were they talking of so earnestly—what, what? The old yearning to know, to understand, returned for a moment, and was followed by an utter blankness; and she knew that she had never known Roddy. He had not once, for a single hour, become a part of real life. He had been a recurring dream, a figure seen always with abnormal clarity and complete distortion. The dream had obsessed her whole life with the problems of its significance, but now she was rid of it.

She had tried to make a reality out of the unreality: she had had the power to drag him once, reluctantly, from his path to meet her, to force a convergence where none should ever have been; and then disaster had resulted. (pp. 352—53)

This inability to distinguish between what is real and what is illusory about people, so convincingly presented in Rosamond Lehmann's first book by means of restricting the reader's access to the story to Judith's awareness, reappears in different forms in all her subsequent novels. But whereas in *Dusty Answer* the lines are more or less clear-cut and Judith's acknowledgement of her infatuation is a painful but positive experience, in the latest novel, *The Echoing Grove*, which deals with adults only, the characters are no longer sure that it is possible to attain a clear notion of what the others are really like. One of the central characters, Dinah, says that in the sphere of feelings truth is practically inaccessible:

I began to dream of shaking it all off [. . .] the whole claustrophobic world of the emotions where truth and falsehood exchange their masks for ever and for ever. (p. 36)

What makes a person real to Dinah is the courage to take a firm stand, what she calls facing a situation. She accuses her sister of being "unreal" and "getting by" in life (see p. 107). Madeleine's fault, according to Dinah, lies in having married Rickie without loving him sufficiently: her own affair with him is only a consequence of this situation. Madeleine is unreal because she does not love enough and refrains from taking decisive steps, while she herself rejects compromises for the sake of truth. But in fact Madeleine is the more sympathetic and humanly warm of the two women. Dinah, whose "contempt for weakness" (p. 107) is evident to Rickie, refuses to accept the weaknesses in him and is trying to make him (as well as Rob, her later lover she is set on reforming) into a person he is not. After many years Rickie sees that

in fact we were all hard at it deceiving ourselves and cheating one another. Dinah too—Dinah most of all [. . .] She would *not* accept we [Rickie and Rob] were no use to her. She claimed if only we tried we could be truly strong; but we wanted to be truly weak. That was a disappointment and a puzzle, but she tried to take it. [She was] so set on learning [. . .] to be wiser, truer than anybody else [and] stronger into the bargain. (p. 267)

Dinah's hardness makes it impossible for her to understand the only man she loves. She is even unaware of a total change in their relationship, when Rickie finally—for the first time—decides to go back to his wife:

Here they were sitting together in one of their old haunts, their hands touching, their voices caressing one another, everything solid, customary, following out its continuity; and at the same time all this *had ceased to have a real existence*. They were shadows, ghosts. It was all in the past, all over. He had stared at her bewildered, wondering why she, so sharp of sight, so hard to hoodwink, should be sitting blindfold opposite to him. She was his clear eyes, yet she did not see what he saw. (p. 115)

There are more instances of Dinah's lack of understanding of the real Rickie. After the sisters' reconciliation and Rickie's death, Dinah talks to Madeleine about his attitude to his Norfolk estate, now sold: "You oughtn't to blame yourself about the place [...] From the way he used to talk about it to me, he didn't miss it" (p. 229). But the reader knows for certain that Rickie missed the place greatly and that the sale meant a cutting off of the roots for him.

Rickie is torn between the love and responsibility he feels for the two women and is forced to practise constant deception in order to keep his promises to both of them. It turns out to be impossible in the long run: Rickie is defeated and his health ruined. Love becomes for him "the game that no one ever won" (p. 125), yet he cannot stop caring till the end, as we see in his conversation with Georgie a few days before his death. Although his love affair with Dinah ended years ago, he cannot but give her up only outwardly: in reality his love for her is as strong as ever and his apparently quiet *pater familias* life only an illusion.

The title of the book reflects both the central idea and the structure of the novel. The "grove" is taken from William Blake's poem which Rickie and Georgie discuss together (p. 256). The grove refers to human passion: "Let us agree to give up love, / And root up the Infernal Grove" ("My Spectre around me night and day")[2]. It echoes in memory throughout the lives of all the characters concerned: passion and love do not cease nor are they transformed (the next two lines in Blake run: "Then shall we return and see / The worlds of happy Eternity.")—Rickie and Dinah do not agree to give up love but are parted at first against their will by his sudden illness at the moment when they decide to go away together. It leaves Rickie with the feeling that the human condition is one of constant frustration, and Georgie adds:

the kind that starts echoes afterwards, backwards and forwards for ever wherever you strike—one echo picking up another till the whole thing *sounds out* like a fulfilment... (p. 231)

The "echoing" of the "grove" of love in the memories of the characters determines the structure of the novel. The central theme in their lives is isolated and presented according to the laws of memory, preserved in the composition of the book (see above, p. 44). Thus the central image of the echoing grove integrates the theme and structure in an intense exploration of such aspects of the experience of love as guilt and innocence, forgiveness and responsibility, strength and weakness, egoism and self-sacrifice and, last but not least, reality and illusion.

The novel that is most explicitly concerned with the theme of illusion and reality is *A Note in Music*. One can speak of three levels of reality in the

---

[2] William Blake, *Poems and Prophesies* (London, New York: Everyman's Library, 1970), p. 342.

story which are transcribed into the world of the novel. There is the reality of everyday facts and events, such as going to the dressmaker or paying a bill. Grace experiences them as the least real:

But what were they—these activities? These were not life. If one could but think cosmically, keep one's mind strained to it even for one minute without collapsing—then one would be brushed by a fleeting intimation of what life was. (p. 309)

The second level of reality is the world of the emotions of the characters, and the third is the reality behind the illusion of both the everyday and the emotional level—of this it is possible to catch only momentary glimpses in sudden moments of vision which are experienced outside time (see above, p. 78). In *A Note in Music* the three levels of reality are merging and only the most sensitive characters try to penetrate the mystery of life, in a way reminiscent of Virginia Woolf:

All that one took for granted was a mystery, all experience meaningless delusion. Truth, could one remember it, wrote naught with everlasting impersonality on all that seemed important [...]
The world is ... is gases blown off the sun and cooling, clotting into systems; and life is infinite millions of atoms and electrons, collecting themselves into millions of shapes of living objects. Life was in all things. (p. 309)

But the third level of reality, the level of truth behind illusion, is seldom explicitly discussed. It is rather suggested by the novel as a whole and by its human context: paradoxically, the technique of subjective vision (in particular the limited point of view) discloses the illusory nature of what the characters often accept as true and (especially through the device of the shifted point of view) the actual state of things emerges.

Rosamond Lehmann in a letter to her brother John drew his attention to a passage in the novel which is "the key to the whole thing".[3] It is a story thought out by Ralph who wants to be a writer:

There were once two lovers who wandered by a pool. They kneeled by the brink and looked down and saw their own reflections. He held her with his arm; she turned her face to his. But, as their lips met, a shoal of fish came darting through the water and shattered their image into a thousand pieces; and when the surface was still again, it was empty of their faces: they were gone.
So in that moment, out of one image of reality three were born: three worlds, or dreams, were made. There was the dream of two happy lovers; and in the pool another dream, where human shadows made symbols of love and life: love wavering and frustrated at the very apex of fulfilment: life scattered and fleeting. And the third was the world of the fishes: beings sentient in their own element, darting from the dark alarm of alien lives into their own separateness again. (pp. 152—53)

The young Hugh Miller is like the fish in Ralph's story: he is unaware of the world he is affecting, the emotions he incites and the image that the other

---

[3] John Lehmann, *The Whispering Gallery*, p. 134.

characters make of him. He is like a being from an alien element into which he returns again, always careful not to get involved, and leaving the dreary town behind with a feeling of relief. He has no inkling what his presence meant to several people.

The two main characters in the novel, Grace and Norah, live chiefly in their past which seems to them somehow more real than the disappointing present. Youth was for them a time of enchantment and expectations which were frustrated in later life. Grace finds her escape in reading novels and going to cinemas; Norah, often against her will, finds herself constantly day-dreaming about her first love, Jimmy. Their present is not real to them, for it is not felt to be quite as significant as the past. Yet they know that there is no getting away from the present, although Grace lets herself dream that

Time was not real, except as one made it so. Why not bind it to one's purpose, make it servant instead of master? It should be a simple matter to abolish ten years of nothingness. (p. 165)

There are other characters in the novel who do not—even to the degree manifested by Grace and Norah—attempt to penetrate the world of appearances and get to the reality lying behind it. They also try to avoid facing their frustrating lives by making up dreams about themselves which give them the strength to go through life. The life of the hairdresser-prostitute Pansy is filled with such dreams of herself and Hugh. She meets him at the town fair:

Follow him, follow him. It was like something on the pictures, all the bustle of the fair, and him the hero going about so heedless, and you the heroine creeping like a shadow after him . . . (p. 214)

When Norah visits Pansy in her capacity of social worker, she is struck by the girl's unreality—pretence and an exaggerated delicacy:

Was it that artifice—dramatization—was the essence of her existence . . . her way of escape from reality, as the psychoanalysts would say? Did she practise an absolute self-deception—seeing herself, in one perpetual day-dream, as the heroine of a series of interesting and pathetic situations? (p. 273)

Norah's intuitions are confirmed by the inside view of Pansy's psyche in the novel. Even Tom, Grace's unimaginative and down-to-earth husband, needs some illusions to compensate for his loneliness and feelings of inferiority. When Grace goes away on her own for a vacation, Tom decides to taste a bachelor's life and begins by going to an expensive restaurant:

He watched his own reflection, raising a wine glass to its lips with dignity and assurance. The large mirror presented all the elements of a restaurant scene in a film—lights, dishes, hurrying waiters—with himself as focussing point—the man of the world, distinguished, solitary, on whom romance was about to centre. (pp. 205—206)

We are reminded of the illusory world, or dream, made by the lovers in the pool in Ralph's story: watching his own reflection in the mirror, Tom finds himself in "a dream, where human shadows made symbols of love and life" (p. 153).

The world of the characters' emotions centres around Hugh and his attractive sister Clare. To Grace Hugh's arrival in the town has proved to be the most important event for years. The first time she saw him she had a feeling of having seen him before—later she found out that in Hugh she recognized a person who was going to mean a lot to her, because he embodied all her frustrated expectations of happiness. She saw him separated from the common grey crowd, in fact different from anybody else she knew: giving out a sense of clear colour (p. 47). Grace could see that his face was not beautiful, but his very person gave her a sense of charm, harmony and joy. Every time she saw him, this joy, a sort of unselfconscious amusement, spread all over her. Hugh became a symbol:

He seemed to have a secret of mastery, of confidence, of being at home in the world. He would disregard inauspicious detail, and be lucky, know how to manage his life as he wanted it (p. 63),

in a word, be all that she herself could not be. She never expected that their acquaintance would lead anywhere, yet his very presence was literally a healing occasion to Grace. After the meeting in the park (Part III) she thought of Hugh and Clare as "bearing gifts": "They had fed a spring inside her, the words had bubbled up from a source long dry. She had been filled with a sense of momentary adequacy as a person..." (p. 90).

Grace becomes dependent on her thoughts of Hugh which provide her with spiritual nourishment. She is able to picture him in his sleep, or in his old age, as she is never to see him in actual life. She asks herself questions about his life and tries imaginatively to fill out the gaps. Hugh is becoming more and more absorbing and mysterious and

she thought with excitement, each meeting seemed purposed, an inevitable step forward, like the development of a play from act to act; and herself at once actor and spectator. Where was she going, powerless, independent of reason, as so idiotically happy? (p. 166)

All the time Grace knows that some day he will disappear from her life irrevocably. She is also acutely aware of the profound difference, not only social, between them. Despite all this it grows to be a working, give-and-take relationship in her mind; Hugh is a living proof to her that happiness is possible, and her never confessed love for him is to armour him against bad luck for life: "This must be her faith, in future, if she was to endure life. She must make herself believe in the spiritual efficacy of her love" (p. 243). Grace's insight and intuition do not tell her anything about Hugh's real state of mind: she sees him rather with his best potentialities realized and it cannot be otherwise from the moment she entrusts the meaning of her life to this symbol. She clings to it with all the strength of her long starved emotions.

Norah sees that her friend Grace

had no important human relationship, occupation or interest—nothing in her life; and yet she herself was in some way a perfectly real person—that is, one capable of experience. (p. 36)

Grace turns away from the outer reality of her life: the ugly town, her dull husband, her feelings of inadequacy, the realization that she has married a man she does not love and thus wronged him for life. Her continual day-dream is of the vicarage where she spent her girlhood and of the countryside in general—they build her only inner reality till the appearance of Hugh. She adds her love for him to it, and, when he visits her for the last time, she strives

to shape herself a lasting image of this meeting. She must make it endure in the infinite void, with inward reality, for the rest of her life; so that his absence, his silence, his forgetfulness—which were to start in another half-hour at most and continue for ever more—should be mere facts of earthly time and space—terms artificial and of no account. (p. 243)

Physical facts can only obscure that inner truth, and thus she assumes an even greater distance towards them.

There is a contrast between Grace's physical solidity, her big and somewhat awkward body, and the delicacy and sensitivity of her spirit. Grace feels the discrepancy and treats her body with a certain carelessness and detachment. When she goes out to the park for the first time after an attack of influenza,

Huddled on a bench, she felt her own breath mysteriously come and go. She heard herself cough: it was the cough of a real person. She looked down and saw herself moored to the seat as firmly as the stout old lady sitting opposite her; yet she felt the wind lift her, whirl her like a straw, a feather, in its wake. (p. 83)

Grace's resigned attitude to her present life and her flight into the sphere of day-dreams is reflected also in her partly feigned indifference to her closest physical surroundings and belongings. Her home is ugly but she takes a certain pride in her own unconcern:

even if her house was dreary and impersonal—at least she knew it [. . .] She did not express herself in royal blue with a frieze, or orange and black stripes, and feel satisfied. It was only that . . . only that she could not express herself at all, in any way—least of all through possessions [. . .] She hated possessions: so she did what was easiest, and then forgot about them. Besides, she was not here really . . . no, she was not here: not in this cage. (p. 14)

Like Grace, Norah is also receptive to the particular aura of reckless enjoyment of life and good luck that seem to emanate from Hugh. He reminds her of Jimmy, a charming dissolute waster killed in the war, who has been her idol for years ("Hugh had appeared in day-dreams—mingling with the other, and wearing his face", p. 292). As in the lives of Grace and Pansy, Hugh fills an emotional void in Norah's world, he grows into a substitute and symbol of fulfilment. She

wished Hugh had not gone away—dear Hugh, so happily at home on earth, looking outward, not always at himself; encouraging one to believe that the gaiety of life had not perished from the world, nor the flavour departed: but had only passed out of one's own reach.

It was extraordinary (seeing how rarely one had seen him), but an undoubted fact, that since his departure there had been a change for the worse in the texture of existence, a failure of elasticity, an onset of aridity. (pp. 274—75)

The irony of the situation is that when we come to the third level of reality, beyond the appearances, it becomes clear that the quickening emotions Hugh and Clare evoke are based on an illusion. Due to the shifted point of view we see that Grace and Norah relate to their own images of him and not to the real Hugh who, behind the delightful and charming manner, is a very ordinary young man, insecure and often depressed. The two women never find this out because their contacts with him never go beyond polite social exchanges, there is no deeper communication between them and Hugh is always on his guard not to get more closely involved. The sense of a purpose in life, which Grace's love gives her, is founded on unreality. There is an incident in the book which expresses this in a figurative way: once on her lonely and happy holiday Grace finds an injured swallow. She takes it home with her and when she wakes up the next day the bird is gone. She

took this for a message, a happy omen. For the first time, she told herself, she had touched something to save, not to destroy it. Now she too would be saved. And the little dream of the bird became mingled with the essential dream of the young man. (p. 192)

But the good omen is an illusion, too. For on the day of her departure from the village she sees the skeleton of the swallow and knows that it has dropped down and never flown away. At the close of the novel Grace is even more resigned, but she still goes on cherishing her own image of Hugh.

Norah, who does not stand as totally alone in life as Grace, is brought back to reality and a sense of proportion as a result of a crisis in her marriage. It is provoked by Gerald's infatuation for Clare and his secret correspondence with her. Norah accidentally finds out about it but when she asks him to let her read his letter to Clare, Gerald categorically refuses. Norah insists, and a violent quarrel ensues, in which Gerald reproaches her for graver disloyalty than his own, that is, for being his wife only on the surface, while passionately loving the man from her past all these years. Gerald realizes that the object of his flirtation is not Clare—the real person, but a symbol into which he has made her, on which centres his attempt to "prove to myself that I could be acceptable—as an individual" (p. 288), and not only as Norah's husband. He has no illusions as to the real nature of

Clare and sees his own motives clearly:

> I wanted Clare's feeling for me at first hand—not just a reflection from your relationship [...] Perhaps I wanted to spite you a little, too. However [...] it had its roots in unreality, so it was bound to fail. (p. 288)

The frank exposure of their grudges and hidden motivation has a salutary, however temporary, effect on the whole relationship of Norah and Gerald. The shock of his well-founded accusations after ten years of a seemingly successful marriage makes Norah see her emotional life in a new, truer perspective—the crisis strengthens their bond.

The theme of the different levels of reality in *A Note in Music* is closely connected with the motif of personal isolation, which seems to me the chief concern of this novel (cf. Chapter IV, Section 2 below). The characters' inability to communicate, and to build their lives on adequate assumptions about one another, results in their flight from reality into the sphere of dreams.

The last of the novels to be considered here is *The Ballad and the Source*, which seems to me the best illustration of the theme of illusion and reality in Rosamond Lehmann. The title itself suggests the subject of the novel: it is a dramatic representation of the relation of the ballad to the source, of illusion to reality. The girl Rebecca comes to know the life story of Mrs. Jardine, told from different angles by a few people. This is the ballad, the most disturbing part of which is perhaps the narrative of Mrs. Jardine herself. Rebecca attempts to find the true picture of Mrs. Jardine, in other words, to get to the source (the other sense in which this word is used in the novel is as the source of life, see p. 124 below).

Getting to the source is not easy, for on the one hand Rebecca's knowledge and understanding are limited, and on the other, there are obvious contradictions between what Mrs. Jardine tells Rebecca and what the child can glean for herself. Ianthe's husband tells his daughter Maisie never to believe anything her grandmother said. Rebecca's own father's opinion is very similar: "She'd charm the bird off the trees" (p. 27), he says and prevents the forming of closer ties between the two families. Yet a few years later Rebecca agrees with Gil that Mrs. Jardine does care for truth, for she remembers her saying: "I will always answer, truthfully, any question you care to put to me. Truth is my foible" (p. 105). And, on the same occasion, "It is sheer idiocy [...] *criminal* idiocy to blinker children, to refuse a decent explanation, or to speak falsely, to pack facts in cotton wool, or smear them with treacle ... or with mud" (p. 105).

At first Rebecca is puzzled by the contradictions she sees in the story:

Two irreconcilable sets of facts confronted me. Miss Sibyl was an authoress [of an autobiographical novel]; she had written something horrid and unkind about

Grandma. Yet, turn the wheel and she was Mrs. Jardine, who loved Grandma so much that her voice altered when she spoke of her; who loved me for being her grandchild. I could only suppose that grown-ups were like that. (p. 92)

There is a certain duality in the personality of Mrs. Jardine which Rebecca promptly notices:

For the first time in her actual presence the sense pierced me directly: that she was wicked. A split second's surmise. But when next moment I looked up at her, there was her profile lifted beautifully above me, serene and reassuring as a symbol in stone. (p. 104)

Soon, however, Rebecca finds a way of reconciling her great attraction to Mrs. Jardine with her sudden premonitions of wickedness in that impressive lady:

It came over me with [a] huge wave of relief and pleasure [. . .] that obviously no person was one and indivisible—one unalterable unit—but a multiplicity; so that every-thing about a person might be equally true and untrue, and I need no longer be puzzled by the badness of good people, and the other way round. (p. 122)

Rebecca loves Mrs. Jardine but at the same time has evidence of Mrs. Jardine's negative traits of character: the girl sees how she boasts, is jealous, double-dealing, proud and egotistic. Even her virtues are not all easy to live with. It strikes Rebecca that

privilege though it would be to be the child of Mrs. Jardine, this status might assume the nature of a formidable burden. So many noble conceptions, so much wisdom and originality, demanding so exhausting a standard of behaviour, presented with such implications of critical reflection upon one's disabilities. (p. 135)

Mrs. Jardine has certain assumptions about herself which, even when repeatedly thwarted, she is not prepared to give up. One of them is her influence over people: she tells Rebecca that she "cannot get accustomed to failure with human beings—particularly the young" (p. 99). Yet she is time and again exposed to this very disappointment. She fails with Maisie, with her best friend Madrona (Rebecca's grandmother), with Tilly, Auntie Mack, Tanya and, above all, with her own daughter, who is driven to insanity by the obsessive hatred and fear of her mother. It is clear to Rebecca that Mrs. Jardine meets nothing but defeat in her long life. She herself views it as a tragedy:

Do you know what goes to make a tragedy? [she asks Rebecca] The pitting of one individual of stature against the forces of society. Society is cruel and powerful. The *one* stands no chance against its combined hostilities. But sometimes a kind of spiritual victory is snatched from that defeat. Then the tragedy is completed. (pp. 107—108)

This clash between a powerful individual, i.e. Mrs. Jardine, and the forces of social convention can explain only in part how her tragedy has started. Since her husband, from whom she had run away, refused to let her take their daughter with her, Mrs. Jardine has become thwarted as a mother, for the law was against her. Further developments, however, are more the result of the drastic methods she employed to encompass her objective than of the "combined hostilities" of society. Her mistake lies probably in her excessive faith in moulding reality after her own designs. The ballad she creates about herself departs too far from reality, and since only a fulfilment of her intentions could satisfy her, she is bound to fail. An example of this is her breach with Tanya, Cherry's governess, who had become a member of the household. As long as she performed the functions assigned to her by Mrs. Jardine, all was well. But when, in Maisie's sarcastic words, "Tanya had had the *extraordinary* vulgarity to fall in love, on the sly, under a real lady's roof, with a piece of a lady's sacred property" (p. 307), namely Gil, the sculptor and lover of Mrs. Jardine's old age, she was immediately dismissed. Mrs. Jardine, as Maisie explains to the shocked Rebecca, was humiliated by her rival's youth and could never forgive Tanya her freedom to marry Gil. Mrs. Jardine chose to ignore the damage she did the girl for whom she was

a person you could always tell the truth to, and she'd understand. That's why she sank down under it so. She could hardly crawl. [Mrs. Jardine, Maisie continues, made] it sound as if she knew everything about [Gil], and they were in a kind of plot together, and Tanya outside, an utter fool and object of their mockery and contempt. (pp. 308—309)

This goes to show how Mrs. Jardine, when she encountered an obstacle, could use her power over people and their trust in her for egoistic and unjust ends.

There are more examples in the novel of Mrs. Jardine' faults, and yet the love and devotion she incites in Rebecca, Gil and others are not wholly unfounded. The responses of the people who love her and of those who hate her are both justified, for each of them possesses a fragmentary truth about her. Rebecca is surprised when Gil tells her that Mrs. Jardine has not much confidence, yet the reader can easily see that her long talks with the girl and the other confidants are symptomatic of Mrs. Jardine's constant attempts at self-justification. Sometimes she defends her dubious actions so fervently that she does not even notice how she contradicts herself. She tells Rebecca about her sending Paul (her very close friend) to Ianthe. When Rebecca innocently asks what Mrs. Jardine wanted him to do, she is almost indignant:

"Want him to do? Oh, my dear child, I am no cunning schemer and plotter. Do you imagine that I exploit human beings for my own ends?" (p. 140)

And, almost in the same breath, she explains her scheme to Rebecca.

Mrs. Jardine has very high expectations from life. She tells Rebecca that she is not weak and not afraid and that her leaving her first husband was the only right thing to do "that could save us from a life of self-contempt and spiritual dishonour [...] I took a step which destroyed his prestige as a man of property. I was his property: he had lost it. Therefore he would destroy me" (p. 110). The course of action that her husband took is perhaps not very different from Mrs. Jardine's treatment of Tanya years later. Yet she seems to be totally unaware of any analogy and firmly believes in her own justice and truthfulness. She belongs to those people "who have an explanation for everything so convincing that it takes in themselves as well as others; who first of all are deceived."[4] In the words of another critic, "Mrs. Jardine victimizes others but she is also the victim of her own delusions."[5] She has created a world picture that conforms with her own ideas but does not make allowances for reality itself—a picture too uncompromising, to which she sticks unconditionally and therefore, despite her insight and love for truth, she ends up deceiving herself. Vida E. Marković maintains that "the delusion embodied in Mrs. Jardine [is] that the role we act in life has just as much reality as our real being, i.e. that the attempt to present ourselves in a different, elevated form is on the whole praiseworthy, motivated as it is by an ideal of human conduct, and that it does neither ourselves nor anybody else any harm."[6]

Once Mrs. Jardine perceptively characterized the young Ianthe for Rebecca as a person who

had built herself a room of mirrors [...] She looked into these mirrors and saw the whole of creation as images of herself thrown back at her [...] She was afraid of the world [...] When people are afraid they dare not look outward for fear of getting too much hurt. They shut themselves up and look only at pictures of themselves, because these they can adapt and manipulate to their needs without interference, or wounding shocks. The world sets snares for their self-love. It betrays them. So they look in the mirrors and see what flatters and reassures them; and so they imagine they are not betrayed. (pp. 119—20)

It is not surprising that Gil, the person best qualified to make objective judgements about Mrs. Jardine, characterizes her a few years later in very similar terms, only this time it is an active way of relating to the world, not a shunning of it:

from anybody else in the world [except her husband Harry Jardine] she gets back—*immeasurable* reflections of herself. It's not deliberate, so it's pointless to moralise about it: it's some property of her nature—some principle, like yeast. She throws out all she has—her beauty, her gifts, her power over people—and objects—and events; and it works. Each time she tries it out, it works like magic. Up come all these disturbing, magnetized self-images. (pp. 236—37)

Gil refrains from any moral judgements and sees this quality of Mrs Jardine's

[4] Vida E. Marković, *The Changing Face: Disintegration of Personality in the Twentieth-Century British Novel, 1900—1950* (Carbondale: Southern Illinois Univ. Press, 1970), p. 110.
[5] LeStourgeon, p. 106.
[6] Marković, p. 98.

as a kind of natural force. Nor does Rebecca take a moral stand towards her and seems to be satisfied with her vision of a human being as a combination of both good and evil tendencies. As Gil and Rebecca admit to each other, they both love Mrs. Jardine and thus they accept her, with her magnificent as well as her sinister traits. And so the reader is not offered any final interpretation of Mrs. Jardine.

Diana LeStourgeon is right in saying that "without doubt this portrait is Miss Lehmann's masterpiece. Mrs. Jardine's very ambiguity insures her hold on the reader's imagination ... Part of her power stems not merely from the complexity but from the elusiveness of her character—from her refusal to be pinned down to any simple interpretation."[7] Time only serves to reveal more facets of Mrs. Jardine, and the ambiguity of her character continues to the very end. It is possible to concentrate only on the moral aspect of her character and view her as a predominantly destructive personality. It seems, however, that the clue to Mrs. Jardine, and the interest of the novel, lies less in a moral evaluation of her often admittedly dubious conduct than in the perplexing interrelation of the ballad to the source.

The recurrent preoccupation with reality and illusion in the novels of Rosamond Lehmann reflects what W. J. Harvey calls "a changed conception of the relation of art to reality, a change largely determined by the modern novelist's sense of increasing alienation."[8] This feeling of alienation in the modern world is an indispensable element in the picture of personal relations in Rosamond Lehmann's books. It will be discussed in the next section, "Personal Isolation".

2. Personal Isolation

A flight from reality into the sphere of illusion is in Rosamond Lehmann's novels almost invariably a result of a feeling of maladjustment, frustration, and disappointment, which in turn lead to isolation. This emphasis on the individual's isolation has a long tradition in the novel which can be traced back to the Romantic conception of man. It is one of the great motifs in modern writing, an important component of what J. Raban calls its leading theme: "If modern fiction has one overwhelming common theme, it is that of the conflict between the individual sensibility and the alien world outside. With such a subject only one point of view is possible—that of the sensitive, and usually suffering, hero."[1] What Dorothy van Ghent says of the point of view in *A Portrait of the Artist as a Young Man* is also true of a great deal

[7] LeStourgeon, p. 106.
[8] Harvey, p. 194.
[1] Raban, p. 35.

of modern fiction, in which "the technique of the 'interior monologue' is the sensitive formal representation of that mental solitude."[2] The point of view of the sensitive hero and the technique of the interior monologue are indeed adopted in all the novels of Rosamond Lehmann. One might say that all her main personages are variations on one and the same character—that of a sensitive girl, a young or a mature woman, and her way of dealing with new experience, usually disappointing, and of surmounting the sense of personal isolation. Moreover, most of the secondary characters also experience isolation of various kinds and degrees.

Allen Tate is struck by this characteristic modern rendering of an isolated individual's condition through his own point of view, so that his alienation from society is shown exactly in terms of his situation:

It is one of the amazing paradoxes of the modern novel, whose great subject is a man alone in society or even against society, almost never with society, that out of this view of man isolated we see developed to the highest possible point of virtuosity and power a technique of putting man wholly into his physical setting. The action is not stated from the point of view of the author, it is rendered in terms of situation and scene.[3]

This is precisely what gives power and intensity to different representations of this recurring theme, for by viewing an individual's isolation through his own point of view we can best comprehend it. Jonathan Raban seems to be right in saying that it is the only point of view possible.

In Rosamond Lehmann's novels we encounter many aspects of personal isolation. There is the isolation a child or adolescent feels when she senses a gap between her own world and the world of adults, and her sense of belonging and security is threatened (*Dusty Answer, Invitation to the Waltz, The Ballad and the Source*). The very process of growing up is often described in terms of the increasing awareness of one's basic aloneness in the world. Hence a manifest nostalgia for childhood, felt by many Rosamond Lehmann's characters who look back on their past as the lost time of youthful sense of harmony with the world, freshness and intensity of sensations (*Dusty Answer, A Note in Music, The Weather in the Streets*). This sense is recaptured by her adult characters in moments of illumination and unity with nature (cf. above, p. 78), though such moments are more often accessible to the young or poetical sensibilities (Judith in *Dusty Answer*, Grace and Ralph in *A Note in Music*, Olivia in *Invitation to the Waltz*). In *A Note in Music* Grace's holiday, the swan-song of her youth, is an attempt at retrieving lost happiness through contact with nature.

There is also estrangement between generations (*Dusty Answer, Invitation*

[2] Dorothy van Ghent, *The English Novel: Form and Function* (New York: Reinhart, 1953), p. 267.
[3] Allen Tate, "Techniques of Fiction", *Sewanee Review*, LII (1944), 223—24.

to the Waltz, The Weather in the Streets, The Echoing Grove), and a sense of class distinctions which precludes or at least makes communication between people difficult (*A Note in Music, Invitation to the Waltz, The Weather in the Streets, The Echoing Grove*). Yet even when such bonds as friendship and love exist, people cannot always permanently silence the voice of their fundamental solitude which, as we shall see in a closer examination of the novels, is present in the experience of a host of Rosamond Lehmann characters.

In *Dusty Answer* Judith's physical isolation and a lack of contact with her contemporaries, except for the Fyfe children, explain to a large extent the intensity of her feelings about them and her inability to see accurately what they are like when deprived of the magnifying glass of her imagination. They fill a vacuum in Judith's emotional life. Before going to college she tells Roddy:

I've never known anyone of my own age except the gardener's little girl and one or two local children—and all of you. After you left, when we were little, I was so lonely I ... You don't know. Daddy would never let me be sent to school. Now you're back, I expect every day to wake up and find you all vanished again. (p. 103)

Judith's absorption in the children next door is reinforced by her estrangement from her mother, an elegant society lady who from Judith's earliest recollections "was more and more away, or busy; and more and more obviously not interested in her daughter. All life that was not playing next door, or alone in the garden, was lessons and governesses" (p. 223). She tried to see herself with her parents

in a relationship of a romantic and consoling sort—an ideal relationship; but then Fred and Mildred would take the place of Mamma and Papa, and shatter the illusion. For they, alas, seemed made of stronger and more enduring fibre: they were real: and they were not often together: and when they were, there was often coldness and now and then quarrelling. Life with Fred and Mildred was neither comforting nor secure. Fred was quite an elderly man, and terrifyingly silent and preoccupied. (p. 227)

When her father, whom Judith loved better than her mother, died, she grieved over him and felt even more alone in the world than before. On receiving the telegram about his death, she considered sharing her unhappiness with her friends next door but, trying to imagine their reaction, gave up the idea, expecting nothing but indifference.

In college Judith is at first terrified by the crowd of unknown girls but soon forms a very intimate friendship with one of them. During the next three years Jennifer becomes the centre of her life and takes the place of the cousins, whom Judith sees only sporadically now. Jennifer is the most beautiful and attractive girl in the college, hospitable, generous, popular and reckless, "drawing them all to her with a smile and a turn of the head, doing no work, breaking every rule [...] flashing the glow of her magnetism suddenly into unlit and neglected lives" (p. 151). With Jennifer as her best friend the sense of isolation vanishes. But Judith is all the time afraid of losing her: "One day when you most needed her she might run away out of earshot, and never come back" (p. 152). It is a prophetic premonition, for this is what actually happens at the end of the novel when Judith, having thrown off her illusions about Roddy, awaits Jennifer in the already unfamiliar Cambridge. Her old friend does not return and Judith is inclined to approve of that decision:

Wise Jennifer shed her past as she went along; she refused to let it draw her back to face its old coils and perplexities and be tangled in them once again. (p. 354)

Now Judith

was going home again to be alone. She smiled, thinking suddenly that she might be considered an object for pity, so complete was her loneliness [...] Yet it was impossible to feel self-pity. (p. 354)

She embraces her loneliness and isolation with a sense of relief, mistaking it for a strength-giving independence:

She was rid at last of the weakness, the futile obsession of dependence on other people. She had nobody now except herself; and that was best. (p. 355)

This is a despondent judgement fitting her mood after the double disappointment of losing Roddy and Jennifer, but the author does not tell us whether she would persevere in it, and guard herself only too well against any future disappointment, turning herself into a replica of her cold mother. Perhaps her bitterness betrays her: she is not as calm and resigned as she believes herself to be. Suffering as she does, Judith is still on the borderline between adolescence and adulthood. The poignancy of her disillusionment is admirably conveyed through the consistent presentation of her vision of all the events.

Judith is by no means the only person in the world of *Dusty Answer* to suffer from loneliness and a sense of estrangement. Almost all the characters experience it: her parents; Jennifer who, as it seems, even seeks isolation; Mabel, another of Judith's college friends—ugly and dull and therefore ridiculed by the other girls; and the cousins themselves, although they are often viewed by Judith as a group with a strong sense of intimacy from which only she is left out.

There is Mariella, who already as a child "spoke little. She was remote and unruffled, coolly friendly. She never told you things [...] She moved among them all with detached undemanding good-humour" (pp. 6—7). Only after many years did Judith learn that at the core of Mariella's inner solitude lay her unreturned love for Julian. Julian was most devoted to his brother Charlie but they quarrelled over his marriage to Mariella and, before they were reconciled, Charlie was killed in the war. This was Julian's permanent cause of remorse which made him lavish his over-protective love on Charlie's posthumous son, without bringing him closer to Mariella. Julian's first-hand experience of the war turned him into a sick man, hating life and unable to find any purpose in it, bitter, lonely and miserable.

Martin, who did not have Julian's sharp intelligence and was not troubled by a sense of life's futility, was forlorn and unhappy for another reason: his hopeless and unceasing love for Judith which, he knew, was never to be returned. And Roddy's potentialities for leading a harmonious and fulfilled life were even smaller, for despite his talent for drawing he was basically indifferent, easily bored, apathetic, and unable to commit himself. Judith herself came to accept her own isolation in a world where it seemed to be an inescapable ingredient of human condition.

In Rosamond Lehmann's next novel, *A Note in Music*, personal estrangement is the most striking and pervasive factor in the lives of most of its characters. Grace, Norah, Tom, Gerald, Pansy, Hugh, Ralph—all suffer from extreme spiritual isolation. Each of them, in his or her particular way, finds it difficult to build successful relationships with their nearest, and, when a stranger comes their way, many of them are liable to make him into a symbol on to which they project their fantasies and dreams of love and happiness. And thus loving Hugh is for Pansy a frustrating experience: she never emerges from her adolescent dreams of a beautiful prince who comes to take her away with him. She is unable to stretch her imagination to meet the stranger, to look for a moment with his eyes. She cannot even try it, for her whole life is built on pretence which enables her to survive the humiliation of her profession and her actual loneliness.

Grace Fairfax, the central and most self-conscious character in the novel, is set apart by her sensitivity and the intensity of her inner life, which stands in contrast to her extreme external passivity. The very same power of imagination which separates her from the drabness of her surroundings makes her secret love for Hugh an enriching experience, even though it has no firm roots in reality. Even a brief encounter with him and Clare in the park made a profound change in her life: "She had been filled with a sense of momentary adequacy as a person; had been enabled to give utterance to little things which were her own" (p. 90). This was a very rare moment in her depressing life in which she felt dislocated in many ways. After her marriage she had to move to an ugly town in Northern England, but could never quite get used to living in it: "The country haunted her still [...] not a day passed without bringing some picture remembered or imagined" (p. 11). In the town

the light had no colour. She thought of the little park [...] None but the saddest, sparsest flowers grew in its beds; and even at midsummer it never quite lost its look of grieving wintry sadness. (p. 21)

Grace's marriage to Tom, the first man who turned up in her life and was kind to her, is also a fact that never ceased to puzzle her, for she knew from the very beginning that it was a mistake. And "though she had taken him and marriage and all for granted long, long ago, she could not quite get used to living with this man" (p. 16). She often thinks about herself and Tom as a couple of strangers. Indeed Tom knows very little about Grace and she is not in the least interested in her decent but dull husband. Their life together is a matter of habit and of keeping up appearances in front of the servant. After the summer holiday they had spent separately, Tom gave up even that and their evenings together passed in silence: "A change had taken place: they were now less strangers than estranged" (p. 238), thought Grace. Even though she finally resolves to make the best of Tom, it is an act of resignation, for there was nothing else to do after Hugh's departure. One night, as Grace was tossing in bed, unable to fall asleep, she was pierced by a realization of the mystery and separateness of each individual life. She was watching Tom in his sleep:

Tom was unfathomable mystery [. . .] She turned and looked at him. She saw the outline of a head upon the pillow—a man's dark head beside her, perfectly still. . . . It might be Tom. It might be Hugh. It might be a stranger. (p. 313)

With the exception of Norah, Grace was completely friendless and socially unpopular. She was happiest on her own, especially in the country, where she often experienced a kind of community with nature that the company of people did not afford. She contemplated nature in a poetical way, although she never wrote a line. Such moments were never shared with anyone else.

A row of hollyhocks bloomed against the fruit wall at the end of the garden. She fancied that their round heads were notes of music painted upon an outspread scroll; chords and scales splashed down in tones of rose and crimson upon the green keyboard of the espalier. Soon, she thought, in the present heightening and harmony of the interplay of all her senses, they would strike audibly upon her ears. (pp. 193—94)

Tom had no idea of this side of Grace's nature. Yet he felt uncomfortably that he was of a different mould and realized that somehow he failed to understand her. "She was deep, was Grace. Sometimes he felt he was positively afraid of her" (p. 202). Their home was always empty, for Grace did not want to entertain; they had never any friends in common. Tom's greatest disappointment in life was that they had no children. When he worked, his life was filled by the office, a Saturday night film, and golf on Sundays. But when he was left alone for his holiday, he was completely at a loss what to do with himself. He wanted to join his wife in the country, and was hurt by her blunt refusal. Loneliness drove him to the fair where he met Pansy:

They stood side by side in the humming and populous solitude, not drawn to each other—not exactly—but inevitably together: the last two people in the world. No need to look before or after. They had nothing to tell one another, and nothing to conceal. (p. 221)

They were brought together by their sympathy for "the Ugliest Woman in the World" displayed in a tent. Feeling dejected and guilty, Tom goes with Pansy for his vapid and joyless little affair.

The other married couple in *A Note in Music*, Norah and Gerald, also suffer from isolation in their marriage caused by the impossibility of facing the truth about themselves and reaching one another. To Norah, her marriage with Gerald meant a separation from her numerous and well connected relatives, who looked on him as socially inferior and difficult. Gerald was Norah's second best choice: for years she had been trying to get over the loss of Jimmy, leading a life of a good mother and patient wife. As we learn in the end, Gerald's injustice and meanness towards his wife were the outer signs of his resentment of the situation which was clear to him, although Norah was convinced that she hid her feelings well. Despite her attempt to remember all the time that "her concern must be with the living" (p. 58), her thoughts were always going back to the past. And when the moment of truth between Norah and Gerald arrived, he flung at her: "You've always left me out" (p. 284).The image of Jimmy in her mind separated them for years.

Norah's loneliness, despite her determination to look on the bright sides of her life, became more acute with Hugh's departure from the town. Yet Hugh himself was not as carefree, well-integrated, and happy as he appeared to be in her eyes. On the contrary, he seems a much duller and less interesting character than Grace or Norah, who envied him. And he was as lonely as they were, especially in the town, where he could find less distraction than he was used to. After his tea at Grace's he went to his unpleasant lodgings and brooded over his bad luck:

For he must admit it to himself: he was not proof against the apalling onslaughts of loneliness. Why had he come back to this damned town on a Saturday evening? Simply on the chance of finding some letters waiting. He had none all the week except for one wretched invitation, and it was unbearable. Everybody had forgotten him. (pp. 65—66)

Thanks to his position, money, and good looks, Hugh managed to enjoy himself in the gloomy town, but he was restless and could not stand it for a longer time. At the end of the novel we see him setting off for abroad. Again he is lonely and melancholy:

there was always a time of loneliness, depression, after the first excitement of the start, the bustle of departure [. . .] A damned awful mood had come over him, amounting to: *Why live?* (p. 314)

He thought of Grace:

108

He had failed again; bungled it somehow. He had never been able to understand himself—much less anybody else. He was a person who would never be able to find any one to confide in—or to love him. (p. 318)

Hugh was devoted to his sister Clare, a young-looking, exquisitely elegant (her taste flattered him), cool and detached woman, who looked down upon her friend Norah's dull life of responsibility and, having divorced her husband, was determined to stay forever alone:

Clare despised her youth and all its storms [...] One goes by oneself, one is free, one enjoys oneself without fear of other people's opinions; one sees to it that no relationship shall sweep one beyond the balancing point where possession of oneself ceases and suffering begins. Yes, said Clare, she could be happy now. (p. 78)

Clare attained peace and satisfaction at the price of loneliness.

The only person who comes near a certain equilibrium in life is Norah's old cousin, Mary Seddon: dignified, loved and respected, content and peaceful, isolated from the noise of the outer world by her deafness. At least this is how both Norah and her grandson Ralph see her. When Ralph was watching these two women together, a sudden realization came upon him which is pertinent to the subject of the whole novel:

All of a sudden, for the first time in his life, it struck him how profoundly each individual life is concealed. In spite of all public indications such as faces, words, actions, the blank persists. Truth is at the bottom of a bottomless well [...] And this commonplace reflection gathered in one second such momentum [...] that he felt that never in his whole life would he be able to seize, reduce, control it. (p. 161)

In *Invitation to the Waltz*, which describes a phase in the emergence of a girl into the adult world, Olivia Curtis lives through the first intimations of her future isolation. A few hours before the ball, the first large scale social event outside her own home, she panics because she dreads isolation among people who, she is certain, will all enjoy themselves:

Why go? It was unthinkable. Why suffer so much? Wrenched from one's foundations; neglected, igonored, curiously stared at, partnerless [...] Oh, horrible images! Solitude in the midst of crowds! Feast from which, a sole non-participator, one would return empty! (pp. 126—27)

The ball is symbolic of the world outside the familiar and reassuring conditions of her present life.

Olivia soon forgets the moments of loneliness at the dance, though when they occur she is naturally greatly distressed. For example, she is bitterly disappointed when she finds out that her sister Kate and their glamorous older cousin from London had gone off gossiping together and leaving her out: "And upstairs they'd run, hand in hand, to have their secrets and be grown up together ... just as in old times, playing Let's run away from Olivia" (p. 219). Presently she thinks of it no more, for she is confronted with

109

a truly and permanently isolated man. When Olivia learns that Timmy had been blinded in the war, a surge of sympathy and protectiveness wells up in her:

> She looked at him, puzzled. Once again he had turned an obvious statement into a question. She looked at him, and in a sudden stab and flash of realization, saw him as one isolated, remote, a figure alone in a far place. (p. 247)

Later she is unhappy seeing him alone, waiting for Marigold who is dancing with a handsome young boy. Olivia asks Timmy to the waltz.

It is her first glimpse of meaningless and genuine suffering, a disturbing example of extreme human isolation. The force of her response to Timmy's lot marks the measure of her own distinctness from the indifferent majority. There are more occasions during the evening when Olivia feels dissociated from her cheerful and well-adjusted contemporaries like the Martins. She has had a long talk with a young poet, Peter Jenkin, nervous, boastful, rebellious, rejecting everything and everybody in a manner that unnerves Olivia. And yet when the Martins and their group make fun of him, she feels that

> If sides must be taken, it was not their side one could take. Of course he was awful [. . .] He was an outcast, made for hatred and derision. But—what was it then that made one feel that, with just a few clues provided, one could get to know him, understand his language? I could soon feel at ease with a person like him [. . .] There must be something shady in me too, then, something decadent. I'm different from them, though they don't know it. She felt the cleavage, deep, uneasy. I'm not going to do the things they'll do. (pp. 213—14)

Olivia is intensely aware of the class differences among the guests and between the Spencers and herself. She feels an intruder when another girl enters the cloakroom for she recognizes in her "one of the house-party; one of the inner circle, the initiated" (p. 263) to whom she does not belong. Later, however, when she meets Rollo outside on the terrace, the peace and silence of the night change her perspective, and suddenly she does not feel uneasy or shy with him:

> Their voices dropped into the air one after the other with an impersonal lost sound, as if they reached one another from a distance; yet the sense of isolation seemed to enclose them together in a kind of intimacy. (p. 273)

This conversation, as we later learn in *The Weather in the Streets*, contributed to Olivia's enchanted vision of Rollo and had important consequences for her life.

Her development in *Invitation to the Waltz* is shown in terms of her growing awareness of one's basic aloneness in the world. Her primary natural integration, her habit of sharing every new experience with her sister, are over: on the morning after the ball Olivia understands that a new phase in their relationship has come, and Kate is not going to confide in her any more. She welcomes her new independence and sense of individuality. When we meet her again in the sequel to *Invitation to the Waltz*, the new freedom she gained has already turned, through disappointment, into a strong sense of personal isolation.

Olivia's presentiment that she was not going to act the way the Martins and their friends would act in life proved true in *The Weather in the Streets*. She separated from her husband and renounced middle class conventional life. She is living among artists and Bohemians, but is not one of them either. By having a love affair with an upper class man she feels that she is doing something against her Bohemian friends. She cannot identify herself with any of these social groups completely.

Olivia has drifted away from her once closely knit family. Her beloved father is weak in body and in mind after a stroke and a severe illness. There is a moment when he looks at her in a way that makes Olivia hope for a possibility of contact with him:

Almost she leaned forward to say: "Dad, are you pretending?"—the notion was suddenly so strong that he was still there, that it was all assumed, out of perversity, laziness, disillusionment: as people decide to be deaf. But the moment passed. He was far out of earshot. (p. 252)

She has never been her mother's favourite, and she knows that this strong woman, with well-defined ideas about right and wrong, disapproves of her conduct. She admires her mother but is not intimate with her. With time the distance between herself and Kate, the approved-of daughter, also grows greater. The kind of success Kate's life represents makes Olivia only sad. Kate is

living an ordinary middle-class family life, valued, successful, fairly contented. One saw her life running, peacefully, unsensationally now on its course, right on to the end: and why did this make one want to cry? Kate isn't wasted. But there should have been something else, I alone know her, some exaggeration. . . . (p. 258)

Her younger brother James, who rebelled against the life expected of him and refused to go into the family business, is on his own and not interested in Olivia's life. She met him once unexpectedly at a London party, and as they talked as two adults she was thinking:

Something's happened to him that didn't happen to his sisters. . . . He'd broken the mould entirely which we were all cast in. Kate might have but she wouldn't—doubting herself and her rebellion, deciding the discipline of ordinary ways was best. I might have, but I couldn't: meeting everybody half-way, a foot all over the place, slipping up here and there, in a flux, or thinking things funny. But he won't do that. (pp. 357–58)

Olivia is both socially displaced and detached from her family, and her love affair only deepens these two kinds of separation. She could not tell her sister about Rollo, because she knew Kate would not approve. Olivia felt guilty from the very start, when she came back from the first party with Rollo: "What luck she was asleep—married, innocent Kate. Tomorrow I shall have grown a more solid mask, there won't be a crack in it" (p. 142). Later, alone and in trouble, she has an urge to confide in Kate, but cannot bring herself to do it.

Being in love makes Olivia withdraw from her circle of friends. At a party without Rollo she was "feeling depressed and lonely, there seemed so much hostility about, and suspicion" (p. 179). She was disgusted and longed to run away from the place:

suddenly I couldn't bear it any longer, I must go to Rollo, there were cigarette stumps and ash everywhere, and empty bottles and marks of dirty shoes, and a pool of something on the oilcloth by the lavatory door, and everybody still going through their dreary old paces. I thought: I don't want them, I'm superior, I've got something of my own, I haven't got to stay. (p. 183)

Only the time spent with her lover seems important: "Not being together was a vacuum" (p. 144). And later, when things did not go as smoothly between them as in the beginning, she tells Rollo:

I haven't much life of my own in between—now—to fill up." I've given up seeing most people; they all think of me as remote now, under a glass case, not mingling with them. They're bored with me. (p. 316)

It was not, however, that communication with Rollo presented no problems. When they saw each other in London for the first time, it was difficult to break the barriers again:

He stood beside me, an elbow on the mantelpiece [...] A stranger. it was all heavy, laborious, flinty, it was like having to break stones . . . wondering: Has he come to unsay it, call it off? (pp. 150—51)

They made love but Olivia was still not assured, "thinking how one's alone directly afterwards" (p. 154). Soon, however, their relationship blotted out everything else in her life and all doubts were allayed. The practical difficulty was that Olivia had to be fitted into Rollo's life in such a way that nobody would suspect him of infidelity. When she went to live alone in a friend's flat for a few weeks, her isolation was almost complete. During the summer, quite unexpectedly, they managed to go away for a short holiday to Austria but even there they had to worry about meeting English acquaintances. Directly after their vacation a nightmarish period of total physical and moral isolation began for Olivia. It was the time of her pregnancy and abortion, while Rollo was in America.

Olivia felt tempted to tell Etty about her predicament, when she was describing her situation as somebody else's and asking her for advice. It turned out that not only Etty but also her other friends had been through this:

Well, well ... She began to feel fatally cosy and consoled, the seals of arduous secrecy, of solitary endurance melting, melting . . . . Not such a catstrophe after all: quite a common little predicament. (p. 239)

But she felt that confiding in Etty and receiving her sympathy would be a betrayal of her love. "She bit her thumb. *I won't.* I can lie and lie; and be alone" (p. 239). Then Etty went away and Olivia, after a short time spent with her parents in the country, came back to London to the empty house:

To be alone, sick, in London in this dry, sterile, burnt-out end of summer, was to be abandoned in a pestilence stricken town; was to live in a third-class waiting-room at a disused terminus among stains and smells, odds and ends of refuse and decay. She sank down and existed, without light, in the waste land. (p. 263)

She spent two weeks alone, going every day after lunch to the park which "seemed populated by seasonal derelics and eccentrics" (p. 265), often people as lonely as herself:

Sometimes she found an empty bench, sometimes she and the others sat side by side in silence, occasionally someone spoke to her, and once started was unable to stop; the dam of isolation down, the spate let loose. (p. 266)

When all was over and Olivia met Rollo after his return to England, she realized that a change in their relationship had taken place. His declaration of love in Austria was not meant to hold true in all circumstances: "We mustn't speak on that scale. When we were in that world we were not in the world. When he spoke such truth [...] he was not true to himself" (p. 324). Olivia told him about the abortion and Rollo was shocked, but not as she expected, "with indignant love and distress for keeping herself from him, not allowing him to help, to share; more as if [...] trying to suppress the extreme of revulsion and dismay" (p. 326). They went for a walk and stood by the river where, in a sudden flash, she understood what was the matter: Rollo's wife was going to have a baby. She felt cheated because it meant that at the time she was happiest with Rollo she actually shared him with his wife. In the same moment when she perceives that she has lost Rollo, she is forced to accept that

We are born, we die entirely alone; I've seen how it will be. To suffer such dissolution and resurrection in one moment of time was an experience magnificent enough in itself. It was far above the level even of the lake, the chestnuts [representing her greatest happiness and communion in love with Rollo]. (p. 330)

In communion with another human being—as in love, or with nature—as in the moments of illumination, one can temporarily transcend the fundamental human solitude which, however, seems to be inescapable in the long run. Olivia's realization of this fact is a complex adult experience, in which resignation blends with acceptance. It differs markedly from Judith's adolescent bitterness.

Soon Olivia was to discover that even when she and Rollo were in love with one another, each meant something else by "love". For Rollo it was only a small part of his life, loving Olivia meant love-making, pleasant talks, and a break from his often gloomy family life. For Olivia, however, it was the substance of her otherwise empty life. Their inevitable separation meant a crumbling of her life's most essential part and going back to living in isolation.

Olivia returns to her friends and after the death of one of them, Simon, becomes once more a member of her circle, all of them mourning him. Now she can see how her closest friend Anna, who loved Simon for years, suffers, and how little the others are able to help her:

Was it merely one's own knowledge of her suffering which seemed to remove and isolate her; or would a stranger also see her as it were behind a veil, scarcely in the room at all? (p. 364)

Anna is isolated by her suffering, as previously Olivia was isolated by her happiness. The major events in life seem to be a matter of individual experience that cannot be shared with other people.

In *The Ballad and the Source* the young narrator Rebecca is an unusually perceptive and sensitive girl; as her French governess tells Mrs. Jardine, "Elle est douce [. . .] et serieuse" (p. 11). These qualities make her an excellent recipient of Mrs. Jardine's remarkable confidences. Rebecca lives a quiet life with a few companions, and this adds to her ability for imaginative concentration on the life story of Mrs. Jardine. She stands a little apart from her contemporaries: when she participates in the celebration of the marriage of Gil and Tanya in the house of the Jardines, they naturally discuss Mrs. Jardine. Rebecca listens attentively but afterwards, when Maisie goes to fetch the pudding and the serious part of the conversation is disrupted, "the circle soon warmed up again and expanded in frivolity, leaving me out of it, eating Christmas pudding" (p. 238).

If the somewhat solitary disposition of Rebecca makes for a stronger impression of Mrs. Jardine on our observer-narrator, it is the character of Mrs. Jardine and the type of personal isolation she represents that are in the centre of our interest here. For paradoxically, this magnetic and powerful woman—having once cast off the conventional life expected of a lady in her position—suffers from social and moral isolation the more acutely the greater her need for love and companionship is. She tells Rebecca that she left her first husband for "there remained nothing but convention to keep us together" (p. 110). She sees her path clearly and never doubts the rightness of this decision, so that the social ostracism which inevitably follows is for her less painful than the later estrangement of Rebecca's grandmother. The loss of her beloved friend, however, is just another consequence of Mrs. Jardine's challenge to the norms of convention which Madrona obeyed: she refused to assist Mrs. Jardine in her atempt to steal Ianthe from her father. Getting Ianthe back became the *idée fixe* of Mrs. Jardine; she has a sense of herself "pitted against a malevolent fate" (p. 130) and reproaches herself for "relaxing my vigilance [...] by forming new ties [i.e. her second marriage] by allowing myself [...] to spread my wings in heedless happy flight, far from my one true dark path" (p. 130).

Following her "one true dark path" she was doomed to loneliness. Her love affair with a young man she ran away with was soon over and then she was left alone and without money. She worked, went to America, wrote a few books and after five years, having saved some money, came back to continue her fight for Ianthe. She kept an eye on her daughter but could not get near her, since her former husband guarded the girl strictly and Ianthe was never left on her own. Mr. Herbert and Ianthe went to live in Florence where he "concentrated his whole being upon two objects; his daughter and his God" (p. 125). Mrs. Jardine speaks with contempt of his perverse love for Ianthe: "Ianthe's father became a singularly abnormal man. Normal people send their energies and emotions through a number of channels. He ceased to do this" (p. 125). Yet her own life was devoted to nothing else than winning Ianthe back. Before his death Mr. Herbert appointed a guardian for his daughter, a clergyman and "a professional understander of women", as Mrs. Jardine contemptuously calls him. Now her fight was with him and when she finally interfered, disaster resulted.

The whole situation alienates Mrs. Jardine from the man she newly married: "in a way I could not confide even in Harry. In a sense, Harry was too simple, too uncompromising a nature to take in what was involved" (p. 139). She hints several times at difficulties between herself and her husband, and there is again a contradiction between the idyllic picture of her marriage she tries to present to the world and her spontaneous confession at another moment: "I am so much alone—I speak so much to myself" (p. 124). She admits her isolation at another point, in a letter to Rebecca's mother, when she writes about Gil: "After many dark years", she wrote, "once more, miraculously, I have someone to *speak to*. I am not dumb by nature!" (p. 215). And inevitably she loses Gil who could not accept for long an arrangement which Maisie maliciously described as one in which

she thought she'd got it fixed up this time good and proper, all serene, everybody revolving round her like dancers round a maypole, without an eye or a thought to spare for anybody else. . . . Oh, she was so sure of Gil! (p. 266)

When Ianthe unexpectedly turns up in the French estate of the Jardines, the dramatic confrontation forced on her by her mother ends in catastrophe: Ianthe is permanently confined to a mental institution. All the people dear to Mrs. Jardine have left her: her favourite granddaughter Cherry is dead; her only grandson killed in World War I; Gil and Tanya left her and got married; Harry, whom Gil called her "resting place", died, curtailing his wife's share in his will, to her surprise.

Harry Jardine is perhaps the most isolated person in the book, drinking heavily and practically never saying a word, while his wife is, in Maisie's words, "blowing him up into a sort of Book of Golden Deeds" (p. 235). His military career was ruined somehow through Mrs. Jardine and he seems totally cut off from other people, especially after the death of Cherry, whom he dearly loved. Mrs. Jardine makes him into an imaginary character of whom she incessantly speaks and "the more he ruined the performance, the more blatantly she'd have to put it over" (p. 235). The young people around her admire Harry for his integrity and Gil declares: "He's not corrupted [. . .] He accepts what's happened to him—in his own way. He doesn't compound with it" (pp. 234—35). The price of this integrity is his total isolation: Maisie compares him to "a locked-up, barred, bolted house you couldn't even be sure was inhabited any more" (p. 233). After the news of his death reached Rebecca, she has a dream of Harry, in which he looks at her with an expression of "a cemented grief, sealing the excavation of an extinct human territory" (p. 317). In the dream he says to her: "She doesn't know anything [. . .] *She can't get in.* She tries it on—but I've got her taped [. . .] Two can play at that game" (p. 318). Despite Harry's total withdrawal during his life, after his death the "Enchantress Queen in an antique ballad of revenge" (p. 238) is left in a still greater solitude.

Personal isolation in *The Echoing Grove* is an essential part of the experience of the characters for whom "personal relations become obssessive".[4] Walter Allen criticizes the novel for being "a suffocatingly claustrophobic work in which never for a moment are we allowed the least relief from the masochistic self-torture suffered by the principal characters. They never transcend their misery."[5] The misery is partly a result of conflicting obligations which Rickie is unable to solve and which lead to mutual estrangement. For years Rickie cannot decide whether to stay with his wife, to whom he is bound by a sense of responsibility, their children, convention and even a feeling of gratitude bordering on love, or whether to reject all this and go away with Dinah, the true love of his whole life. This false position produces a curious split in Rickie's personality, for, as he continues to live a double life, he is forced to turn a deaf ear to a part of his self, in order to preserve his sanity. His tragedy lies in the fact that for the most part he heeds both voices, and when he finally renounces Dinah (or circumstances force him to do so), a part of him dies. There is in the book a recurring image of Rickie as a caged being, unable to extricate himself from the dilemma (see p. 56). He is caged and divided when Dinah asks him for help that he knows he must not give if he is to remain loyal to Madeleine (p. 132). Dinah sees a split in Rickie at the time when they part for good. Watching him run downstairs in his characteristic

[4] Walter Allen, *Tradition and Dream* (London: Phoenix House Ltd., 1954), p. 196.
[5] Ibid.

unbroken skidding run from top to bottom of the staircase [...] it struck me with a pang that what I witnessed was a man dividing: a schoolboy giving me the slip went hurrying down ahead, improving his technique; abandoning upstairs a stock-still man with heavy shoulders. In the void of this split husk he left me cancelled ... (p. 43)

Rickie hurries back to his wife, for they are invited to a party. When he gets home to Madeleine, he notices with distaste her evening dress and overdone make-up:

She was beginning to plaster it on, he thought, like the rest of them. All but one, one pale one. White moth among Painted Ladies, quite out of place in this our life. Brush her off, let her fly or fall ... Too late. Can't be done. Impaled, look, wing-stretched, stiff, a long sharp pin through her ... through me, impaling me. (p. 47)

Thus torturing himself with the thoughts of Dinah, he pays a compliment to Madeleine about her appearance, and lies to her about the cause of his delay. Then their taxi comes and "in close sad separation they went" (p. 50) to the party. The mockery of the situation is that the party has been arranged by their friends in order to celebrate their coming together, whereas Rickie is as far as he could be from Madeleine that night, tormented by his inability to respond to Dinah and help her in any way.

During the party everything seems to Rickie "meaningless, two-dimensional, like figures on a film screen, on the other side of the glass prison in which they sat together" (p. 67). They both pretend everything is all right but after a while Rickie cannot endure it any longer and, provoked by Madeleine, abruptly leaves the party:

he became disconnected. He was now an automaton, a man-machine, enabled to record but not to correlate, let alone feel, a variety of sensory impressions. For instance, two curiosities: Madeleine stretched a peahen neck and pecked at his dry heart. The wrenched-off head of Dinah swirled away. (p. 240)

Madeleine is enraged and helpless. Rickie comes home hours later, goes into her room and sits on her bed,

simply null and void, as if he had been washed up somewhere by a broken dam [...] as indifferent to the moral challenge, or to the rudiments of etiquette, as a babe new-born. Above all, out of reach—stubbornly so: as if his will had operated a deliberate assumption of irresponsibility; an absolutely ruthless withdrawal into self-preservation. (pp. 75—76)

Nevertheless, now they begin to talk the situation over and are brought together again, although they both know they cannot alter the fact that it is Dinah Rickie loves, not Madeleine. And yet it is Madeleine's triumph, for Rickie is to stay with her. Dinah, at least for a time, is out of the picture.

Rickie's technique of withdrawal (demonstrated in the scene with Madeleine) has been his characteristic way of dealing with situations he cannot solve. The first time he resolves to break with Dinah and, failing, confesses it to Madeleine, he lets himself feel

117

like a person coming round from chloroform. No use for the nurse to bridle, flounce, scold, weep, coax, cross-examine: he was entirely excused; she simply had to take it.

"Shall I go and see her?" said her voice, at last, from afar; and he replied, at last, from an equal distance:

"Would that be a good idea?" (p. 122)

He leaves the initiative in Madeleine's hands, and is grateful to her for taking over. But shortly afterwards, when Madeleine goes away to visit her sick father in South Africa, he sees Dinah again. At her request he takes her for a short holiday, at the end of which they decide to leave England together. On her return Madeleine immediately senses the change in Rickie and, not for the first time, thinks: "It was all over. She was alone with a stranger" (p.139).

Thus their marriage oscillates for a long time between the constant threat of breaking up and temporary periods of truce and apparent peace. They live for the most part as strangers, isolated or estranged from one another. Madeleine loses her self-confidence and, at one point, wonders if her wearing veils so often "could be connected with the psychology of rejection" (p. 185). Although their marriage survives, in the years that follow "all they can give each other is remorseful pity [. . .] Such cold comfort" (p. 61)—as Georgie writes to her husband. As for Dinah, the cause of the conflict, she is left stranded, lonely and without "an emotional focus" (p. 196), fighting for a long time in order to transcend her unhappiness and learn to live with her own independence.

Rickie is not only estranged from his wife. In his contact with other people there is always an element of secrecy, he is on his guard. Even when he tells Georgie the story of his life, she feels she cannot get close to him in spite of all his sincerity:

He turned his head on the pillow to look at her and smile; yet [. . .] the structure of his face seemed to express more of austerity than tenderness, his almost closed eyelids less of union than of separation, distance. (p. 237)

And even after they have made love, Georgie feels that somehow she cannot touch him, for he has for years lived in a growing separation from the world. During their very long conversation he even speaks at times about Georgie in the third person, as if he were alone, objectively considering her point of view (p. 279). Yet she can see that he is not indifferent to everything. He cares about his moral standards, what he calls "trying to be good" (p. 254), and he says: "I hope I'll die before I start forgetting to feel uncomfortable" (p. 255). Rickie's moral principles make him lead a life of increasing isolation; in the end he retires more and more often from home, not wishing to be in Madeleine's way. She in turn is finally abandoned by her lover, and is left more completely alone than at the time when she lived with Rickie who, after all, did care about what happened to her.

The loneliness of Georgie is of a different kind, for she is an exile in

England. Moreover, she fell in love with Rickie the first time she saw him, just before she married his best friend. During their last meeting Rickie, in a moment of insight, sees

as if he had touched, separated, and held it up before him, a core of isolation in her, a shape coldly illumined, contained, defined, like a dark crystal with a grain of incandescence in its heart. (p. 218)

It is perhaps this recognition that enables him to reveal himself so fully to her, after a long time of silence.

Two other men with whom Dinah was involved after Rickie are even more lonely and maladjusted than herself. One of them was a young lower class extremely good-looking man who made his living by preying on rich people and whom Dinah unsuccessfully tried to reform. He seemed to Rickie

to have the look of an Incurable ... that kind of unnaturally separated, fastidiously sterile sort of aura. You saw him pushing his plate away, or throwing up what he couldn't swallow—which was the human race in general [...] And yet there was such sadness in him—the sadness of a creature in the ZOO—irremediably displaced. (p. 264)

The other man was another exile, a Jewish doctor from Germany, who was responsible for the death of the woman he loved. When Dinah came to him for drugs (she wanted to commit suicide), he dreamed of giving her her life, and with it his love, instead of death. The situation did not develop in the way he imagined, and he committed suicide just before the outbreak of the Second World War. Dinah tells Madeleine about him:

I had the obsession once that I was the loneliest person in the whole world; but he cured me of that. He really was lonely—irremediably lonely. In the way pariahs are—pariah dogs. (p. 318)

In The Echoing Grove the whole gallery of these isolated people, apart from being involved with one another in a direct or indirect way, have one thing in common: their ultimate personal isolation results from an inability to enter successful interpersonal relationships. The reasons for this are many, among them a sense of a more general spiritual dislocation in the world, of a fragmentation of life that cannot be allayed by loving an individual man or woman. The narrative technique of the novel, with its irregular movement from one consciousness to another, enhances the general effect of fragmentation.

3. Fragmentation of Life

Virginia Woolf referred to the time in which Rosamond Lehmann's novels were written as the "season of failures and fragments".[1] By this she meant that individuals lost their sense of living within a structure of a certain stability. She discussed the impact of this loss on writers and what she said about contemporary fiction in the twenties is often true of the novels of Rosamond Lehmann. Let us consider one of them from this perspective.

In *Invitation to the Waltz* (1932) the excitement, anxiety and delight of a seventeen-year-old girl's first ball are brilliantly grasped and recorded. And yet, even though "the experiences of childhood and adolescence are more vivid than our own, their joys and sorrows sharper, their perceptions more acute",[2] and the book is successful in many ways, one would hesitate to call it truly great literature. For, as R. Wellek and A. Warren put it,

we are content to call a novelist great when his world, though not patterned or scaled like our own, is comprehensive of all the elements which we find necessary to catholic scope or, though narrow in scope, selects for inclusion the deep and central, and when the scale of hierarchy of elements seems to us such as a mature man can entertain.[3]

Now *Invitation to the Waltz*, belonging certainly to literature narrow in scope, does not include "the deep and central". This is the plight of much contemporary fiction which, according to Virginia Woolf, leaves us with a "sense of promise unachieved : .. of brilliance which has been snatched from life but not transmuted into [great] literature".[4]

Why is this so? Virginia Woolf saw the answer in the changed situation of the modern artist. In older writers, like for example Jane Austen, "there is the natural conviction that life is of certain quality. They have their judgement of conduct. They know the relations of human beings towards each other and towards the universe."[5] But most modern writers have ceased to believe in such an ordered universe. Because they do not believe that their impressions of life hold good for other people, they can do no more than speak about their own individual experiences; they cannot "be released from the cramp and confinement of personality".[6] Thus in Jane Austen "the little grain of experience once selected, believed in, and set outside herself, could be put precisely in its place, and she was free to make it ... into that complete statement which is literature."[7] Yet in a very gifted modern writer

---

[1] Virginia Woolf, "Mr. Bennett and Mrs. Brown", p. 110.

[2] Dangerfield, 175.

[3] René Wellek and Austin Warren, *Theory of Literature,* p. 214.

[4] Virginia Woolf, "How It Strikes a Contemporary", *The Common Reader*, p. 300.

[5] Ibid., p. 301.

[6] Ibid., p. 302.

[7] Ibid.

like Rosamond Lehmann the "grain of experience" is not set outside herself and put in a perspective. One might say that though she captures "the grains of experience" beautifully, she is in turn captivated by them and therefore often confined, in the words of G. Dangerfield, to "a world at once delicate and obtuse, a world whose emotions are exquisite and whose exclusions are innumerable, a world where the major issues of fiction have no place at all."[8] Rosamond Lehmann says of these "grains of experience" that "there is not one of these fragile shapes and aerial sounds but bears within it an explosive seed of life."[9] Yet the author herself is only a passive instrument who does not order her experience according to either some well-defined hierarchy of values or a dynamic principle, but is "as a kind of screen upon which are projected the images of persons—knows well, a little, not at all, seen once, or long ago, or every day; or as a kind of preserving jar in which float fragments of people and landscapes, snatches of sound."[10]

The restriction of many modern writers' perspective to the subjective, with no attempt at offering more general statements about life, has been fairly common in "a time of shocking disclosure of the failure of the social environment as a trustworthy carrier of values".[11] The transitional quality of our age is felt by most creative artists. Although one can see a similarity between Henry James's *What Maisie Knew* and Rosamond Lehmann's *The Ballad and the Source* (cf. above, p. 21), many of the substantial differences between the two novels can be attributed to the different social climate in which the two novelists lived. Maisie's straightforward and innocent bearing has wider implications: she is, in James's words, "really keeping the torch of virtue alive in an air tending infinitely to smother it."[12] In *The Ballad and the Source* there is no such unequivocal moral situation. The objectives of the two novels seem to be different: James is concerned here above all with an ethical problem—the confrontation of innocence with corruption and the formation of Maisie's "moral sense". Rosamond Lehmann's preoccupation lies more in the purely psychological sphere which reveals simply how the characters are trying to come to terms with their condition. What matters, in other words, is an intricate texture and not a moral order of experience.

Although Rosamond Lehmann used a technique originated by James in her treatment of a similiar theme (a child's first encounter with the evil and corruption of his elders), its framework, as we have seen, is quite different in the two novelists. Rosamond Lehmann's concern is with the true nature of

---

[8] Dangerfield, 175.
[9] "The Red-Haired Miss Daintreys", in *The Gypsy's Baby* (London: Collins, 1946), p. 57.
[10] Ibid.
[11] van Ghent, p. 263.
[12] Henry James, *What Maisie Knew*, preface, p. 4.

the very process of living as it is experienced by her heroines. The question is: what is the meaning of this experience? Is there a pattern in it? What is the essence of life? These fundamental questions—a conspicuous concern of modern fiction—are reflected in Rosamond Lehmann's writing:

I don't know whether it's mere chance, or if it's because in old days people were born with the secret—and now have lost it—but I can recall no historical instance of inquiry into the subject of life. What is truth?—What is love?—but never, till now, What is life? It is not my voice but the voice of Virginia Woolf that I hear asking the question.[13]

Both the works of Virginia Woolf and those of Rosamond Lehmann are examples of how, as David Daiches says, "the novelist unconsciously rationalizes an impulse which comes, not from some personal discovery in style or technique, but from the state of civilization."[14] The often discussed collapse of the old values and institutions, the typically modern sense of living in a fragmented, confusing and insecure world, have resulted in a need of self-definition, a search for some objective reality, and a new realism for expressing it.

The typical protagonist of modern fiction—a sensitive individual confronted with an indifferent or hostile society—suffers from the loss of a centre in life and from personal isolation. Such are the heroes of Rosamond Lehmann who, moreover, admits this lack of a centre in herself as a creator:

I am nothing but a screen for chaotic images—images assembling, blurring, dissolving—a crazy cinematograph, with here and there an attempt at synchronization—husky indifferent records of other people's voices, fragmentary echoes of laughter and weeping.[15]

The reality with which Rosamond Lehmann is primarily concerned in her novels is that of individual sensibility. What has been written about Elizabeth Bowen can be easily applied to Rosamond Lehmann's novels: "the prime technical characteristic of her work, as of other modern women writers, such as Virginia Woolf, is that she fills the vacuum which the general disintegration of belief has created in life by the pursuit of sensibility. It is a highly sophisticated pursuit."[16] In Rosamond Lehmann the pursuit is "unconventional" for "she writes of romantic heroines in an age that has made the two words pejorative."[17] Elizabeth Bowen, who is full of praise for *The Echoing Grove,* appreciates this quality in particular. She writes in her review of the book that Rosamond Lehmann "has been so bold, in our time, as to picture the absoluteness, the entirety of love—its power to consume

---

[13] *A Letter to a Sister* (London: The Hogarth Press, 1931), p. 21.
[14] Daiches, p. 224.
[15] *A Letter to a Sister*, p. 15.
[16] Sean O'Faolain, *The Vanishing Hero* (New York: Books for Libraries Press, 1957), p. 167.
[17] Ibid.

persons, and to consume itself."[18] When Rosamond Lehmann depicts the disillusionment of her romantic heroines sympathetically, she is "bold" to do so in our time, but when one of them (Olivia in *The Weather in the Streets*) says: "We're hollow people" (p. 331)—and such moods are expressed quite often in Rosamond Lehmann's novels—then we immediately recognize "an impulse [coming] from the state of civilization."

Whereas Rosamond Lehmann is concerned solely with individual sensibilities and fates, and one could hardly call her a socially committed writer, her novels, in so far as they reflect the spirit of the times, inevitably comment on the contemporary world. As W. Harvey remarks, "It is within ... this mashing together of individualities, that [the characters] preserve their autonomy, yet through our perception of the pattern their significance extends beyond themselves into a general comment on the world."[19] One such comment that emerges from her novels is a sense of the decline of social norms to which she gives expression more directly in *A Letter to a Sister*: "Society isn't what it was surely, it has lost its glamour in the nursery; the thrill of virtue and wickedness is less, rewards and punishments are out of fashion?"[20]

In one novel after another we see how the old systems of values are questioned, religious or filial feelings disappear, and no new satisfactory norms take their place. Love between man and woman becomes the pivot of life, and, when it fails or is thwarted, people lose their centre of orientation in life. Individual morality no longer is a sure guide in life, for it has ceased to be universally accepted. In *The Echoing Grove* Rickie, who feels responsible both for his wife and his mistress, knows that his own code of decency belongs to the past:

It's not that they [the new generation] behave any worse than our sort—my sort—on the whole: it's just that they don't behave at all. Behaviour has ceased to be a concept. I've got a hunch they simply don't know what it feels like to feel disgraced [...] You could say it was innocence, lack of humbug—and of the code of the Decent Fellow and high time too. Seems to *me* more like something left out, subtracted ... like a dimension missing almost ... (p. 243)

The sense of change and decline is evidenced both in the individual fates of Rosamond Lehmann's protagonists and in her description of the characters who are primarily types only, usually representatives of a certain social class. *The Weather in the Streets* may serve as an example here, for its characters embody, in various ways, the idea of a world in decline. The decline can be perceived all the more clearly when it is seen against the background of the same world ten years before, in *Invitation to the Waltz*. There is the

[18] Elizabeth Bowen, "The Modern Novel and the Theme of Love", *New Republic* CXXVIII (May 11, 1953), 19.
[19] Harvey, p. 69.
[20] *A Letter to a Sister*, p. 7.

dressmaker Miss Robinson who, after long years of spinsterhood and life with her cheerless family, lost her former good spirits and succumbed to a nervous breakdown; there is Major Skinner, who had, in vain, tried to befriend the Curtis girls (because of his wife, a woman with a past, he was not accepted socially), now he is dead from a cold caught during his affair with a local girl; there is Timmy, the beautiful blind man whose dignity once impressed Olivia, now willingly dying of consumption. Marigold, once so full of life and exuberant, is bored with life, unhappy and drinking. Her own deterioration is accompanied by both personal and financial troubles in her family. At the Spencers' dinner party Olivia sits next to Sir Ronald, a comical and exasperatingly ardent defender of the good old times, who deplores the end of all aesthetic standards and the hardships of the upper class families like the Spencers. Olivia carefully agrees with him that "it's the end of a chapter" (p. 84). Sir Ronald is unaware of her lack of enthusiasm for the old order. In fact Olivia is the black sheep of the family because she has rebelled against the approved way of life expected of her: she is a victim of the disintegration of the values of the older generation. "A life of belief" is no longer possible for her, or for her brother James and her Bohemian friends, and the atmosphere of sterility in which she lives is dispersed only momentarily by her abortive love affair.

The fragmentation of life, which is depicted so concretely in *The Weather in the Streets* in terms of the realities of the London life between the wars, is expressed more figuratively in *The Ballad and the Source*. Its action takes place mainly before the First World War and a sense of an impending change for the worse in the world is only vaguely felt by the young Rebecca. Thinking about her grandmother, the grown-up Rebecca reflects:

It was this [energy with a core like the crack and sting of a whip] that had left our house, and perhaps most similar houses at that period. There were no words for it, of course, one might express it by saying there seemed disillusionment lurking, unformulated doubts about overcoming difficulties; a defeat somewhere, a failure of the vital impulse. (p. 15)

The decline is transcribed in the life of Mrs. Jardine, whose defeat and disillusionment are due to frustration of the vital impulse. She describes for Rebecca what she means by the source of life:

The fount of life—the source, the quick spring that rises in illimitable depths of darkness and flows through every living thing from generation to generation. It is what we feel mounting in us when we say: "I know! I love! I *am!*" (p. 101)

As long as the source is unimpeded, human beings can love and lead integrated lives. When Mrs. Jardine later tells Rebecca that sometimes this source is vitiated, she unwittingly describes herself. Rebecca can observe how the next two generations come to pay for this impairment. Yet her admiration for Mrs. Jardine, as well as for her own grandmother, continues, and she cannot help feeling that they have no equals in her own generation.

The decline of vitality and self-assurance in the younger generation as compared to the older one is illustrated more fully by the children-parents relationships in *The Weather in the Streets* and *The Echoing Grove*. It is also significant that the first readers of *Dusty Answer*, as John Lehmann testifies, "looking for something that would make articulate and put into perspective the experience and feelings of our own generation, our sense of being cut off from the past by the war and endowed with unique sensibility and revolutionalized values we did not expect our parents' generation to understand ... agreed with me and found that Rosamond had spoken for them as no one else had."[21] All the more sensitive characters in the book are somehow dislocated in the world and have lost a sense of belonging and rapport with the generation of their parents: they stand practically alone in the world, not supported by their elders. In *The Weather in the Streets* and *The Echoing Grove* (which is often repetitive of *The Weather in the Streets* in its treatment of the generation gap) the contacts are stronger, and so is the conscious opposition against the life represented by the generation of the parents.

In *The Echoing Grove* Dinah, the rebel of the family, discusses these problems with her mother, Mrs. Burkett. It is during the War, after Rickie's death whom his mother-in-law deeply loved and considered "her spirit's son". She feels that neither of her daughters really understood and appreciated him, and she is irritated by Dinah's sociological generalizations about his position in the modern world. Mrs. Burkett valued Rickie for his goodness and did not censure him for his weakness:

It was not a broken life and not a failed one, she declared passionately to herself: he had chosen it with his eyes open and completed it [...] her children ridiculed her code and gave her to understand that the facts of life were still concealed from her. One simple fact had never crossed their minds, the fools: she understood men and they did not. She had not lost the instinct for the art of sex, inherited from her mother and grandmother. [...] But nowadays they were bent, all of them, on fulfilling themselves with the aid of textbooks: every bodily and mental function explained, explored and practised with business-like thoroughness and zeal. All very well, all very sensible ... but oh! deplorable. So much frankness and obtuse perversity, so much enlightenment and atrophy, so much progress and *dégringolade*. (p. 159)

She remembers with disgust the letter Dinah wrote her after her husband Jo had been killed in Spain, "that dreadful document, setting out firm valid reasons for marching on breast forward, never doubting—placing the enlargement of my political horizon before her private grief ..."(p. 155). Mrs. Burkett does not approve of Dinah's way of life either: "she is *mal entourée*, hobnobs with riff-raff, people with opinions and no breeding, always has" (p. 155). She cannot totally accept Dinah's view of the modern situation which her daughter presents to her with strong conviction:

[21] *The Whispering Gallery*, p. 131.

if ever a generation knew its own strength [Dinah tells her mother] it was yours: or rather *didn't* know it, as the saying goes, meaning it's so tremendous it hasn't got to be consciously considered, for good or ill. We inherited your Juggernaut momentum; but of course not your sphere of operations. (p. 160)

Rickie's situation, according to Dinah, was even more difficult because

he was a romantic orphan boy, irrevocably out of the top drawer. He was never at home in his situation, was he?—I mean the contemporary one, the crack-up—not just the general human situation of wondering why you're born. (p. 160)

Mrs. Burkett cannot bear Dinah's cold and opinionated way of discussing Rickie and, to her daughter's unpleasant surprise, reminds her of the event that took place years before and which summarized the modern priggishness that she detests:

Well do I remember, though his name has mercifully escaped me, some youth, I believe he styled himself a writer [...] "You see, Mrs. Burkett," he said to me—so graciously of him!—in the course of conversation, I was trying, I dare say, to discover his aims and interests—"You see, Mrs. Burkett, the fact is Western civilization is in *decline* and those of us like *myself* who are *aware* of it must reflect it in our *lives* before crystallizing it in our *work*. We cannot be expected to *behave*." (p. 167)

Mrs. Burkett evidently despises this reasoning, so contrary to her own norms of conduct.

The concept of behaviour, the necessity of knowing what is right and what is wrong, emerges once more in the novel, towards the end, after the death of their mother, when the reconciled sisters spend a weekend together. Trying to console Madeleine, who cannot understand why her lover abandoned her, Dinah analyses the modern woman's situation:

I can't help thinking it's particularly difficult to be a woman just at present. One feels so transitional and fluctuating ... So I suppose do men. I believe we *are* all in a flux—that the difference between our grandmothers and us is far deeper than we realize—much more fundamental than the obvious social economic one. Our so-called emancipation may be a symptom, not a cause. Sometimes I think it's more than the development of a new attitude towards sex: that a new gender may be evolving—psychically new—a sort of hybrid. Or else it's just beginning to be uncovered how much woman there is in man and *vice versa*. (pp. 311—12)

Even if Dinah comes to admire her mother's moral code, it is impossible for Mrs. Burkett's daughters to follow it, for the situation has changed. Dinah departs early from her mother's norms and makes use of the new freedom to experiment with her life and mould it into a new pattern. She does not blame anybody for her defeats, and in the end accepts responsibility for her actions.

In this context, the importance of childhood as a phase of one's primary integration into the world stands clear. It is characteristic of Rosamond Lehmann's novels that youthful disillusionments lead to growing anxiety and

126

isolation of the individual. This isolation is connected with an inability to sustain personal relationships whose central place in human life is implied in all the novels. It is affirmed in *The Echoing Grove*, for example, in Georgie's letter to Rickie's daughter Clarissa, after his death: "We talked for a long time not about the War but about really important things—people, human relationships, personal feelings ... " (p. 289). The most prominent among these relationships is sexual love. As a modern psychologist remarks, due to a general dislocation in the modern world, it has "come to carry the weight for the validation of the personality in practically all other realms as well."[22] The novel illustrates how this, seemingly the only way of integration in the all-pervading fragmentation, proves to be an insufficient basis for existence.

It can be safely said of the novels of Rosamond Lehmann in general that they are a happy combination of modern techniques with the substantial traditional portrayal of the individual as a social being, however small the group of people represented may be. The protagonists are always firmly placed im their social context, which is a dimension of character that enhances its reality: "one of the things which makes for substantiality of character in the novel", writes Lionel Trilling, "is precisely the notation of manners, that is to say, of class traits modified by personality."[23] Rosamond Lehmann has, in my opinion, avoided the dangerous situation which in Virginia Woolf's fiction developed "in the direction of a greater and greater concern with the sensibilities of her characters, less and less with their lives as social beings."[24]

In John McCormick's opinion, Rosamond Lehmann

may be said to have begun where Katherine Mansfield and Virginia Woolf left off. Sensibility for [her] is not an end but a means; in this area experiment continues to take place, not dramatic experiments in technique, but experiments in the possibilities of human communication which utilize earlier techniques. *The Echoing Grove* is firmly rooted in English society of the last thirty years; it is an explicit novel of manners, as well as a novel of sensibility and a novel of ideas ... As in Miss Lehmann's earlier novel, *The Ballad and the Source,* the unifying theme is the fragmentation of Victorian and Edwardian social patterns from 1914 to the present.[25]

One might add that this is the unifying theme of all the novels of Rosamond Lehmann, and her interest in manners, concern with conflicting moral codes, and acute observations of class differences and snobbery (much in the nineteenth-century tradition) are in evidence from her first novel to the last. These general ideas are always expressed in terms of a character whose

[22] Rollo May, *Love and Will* (London: Collins, 1972), p. 60.

[23] Lionel Trilling, "Art and Fortune", in *The Liberal Imagination* (New York: Doubleday, 1957), p. 253.

[24] Mark Schorer, *The Novelist in the Modern World* (Tucson: Univ. of Arizona, 1957), p. 15.

[25] McCormick, *Catastrophe and Imagination*, p. 89.

experience governs the novel, and not the other way round, as in some traditional novels, where character serves to illustrate a moral point about man in society. When, for example, the theme of war appears, it is accomodated in the experience of the heroines (Olivia's in *Invitation to the Waltz*, Dinah's in *The Echoing Grove*) and thus made real, looming, as it were, in the background and shown only in its disruptive effects on people not directly involved. Similarly, *The Weather in the Streets*, apparently concerned with a purely private world of emotions, through a lack of detachment towards interwar London life, gives an authentic picture of the times. A faithful representation of the fully realized character of Olivia Curtis involves an image of contemporary manners which gives to this love story an almost documentary quality.

John McCormick calls Rosamond Lehmann a "cognitive novelist", i.e. a writer

who has encompassed with his mind the order-defying history of our time, and he has in addition comprehended and accepted that history with his emotions to the degree that he is able to project his dual comprehension meaningfully in the novel ... in the cognitive novel, ideas, character and situation become meaningless if we attempt the operation of removing from their total dimension the objective framework of idea in which the characters live and have being.[26]

McCormick chooses *The Echoing Grove* as the book illustrating his category of the novel of cognition. Not only does the novel hinge "upon the realization of individual, private sensibility, and at the level of sensibility ... succeeds totally; [it is also] a study of the failure of marriage and of the nature of love in a fragmented society."[27] The distinction of the novel lies in its "ability to transcend sensibility, to reach into our society and to tell us something about ourselves."[28]

The novels of Rosamond Lehmann well illustrate how the general instability and fragmentaion of modern society affects the quality of relationships between people. When Olivia's love affair with Rollo (*The Weather in the Streets*) comes to an end, she has nothing to fall back upon. Neither her family nor her friends, themselves "in a muddle", can offer her much in the way of gaining a foothold in life. The powerful attraction that Lady Spencer exerts for Olivia consists in the fact that Rollo's mother, standing for tradition and convention, possesses a certainty of right and wrong which gives her an enviable strength. As a girl (*Invitation to the Waltz*) Olivia

adored her for her sober splendour, for the sense of lofty moral principle, of masterful beneficence, of affectionate despotism which she diffused. [Olivia] feared

---

[26] Ibid., p. 85.
[27] Ibid., p. 86.
[28] Ibid.

her for her eye, hawk-sharp to spot such details of appearance and behaviour as displeased her; for her tongue, unsparing to denounce offenders. She was always right. She knew it. (p. 155)

Years later, when Lady Spencer comes to Olivia to entreat her to break the relationship with Rollo, Olivia fights her with all her might. She is desperate to the point of rudeness and yet knows throughout that trying to ascribe cynical motives to lady Spencer is unfair and that her judgement of the situation is probably better than her own. There is a moment in their conversation when

the old feeling came surging up. Lady Spencer, I'm in trouble, help me. You know everything. Beloved benefactress, infallible . . . Punish and forgive me, approve of me again. Say: I knew my Olivia wouldn't fail me. (p. 282)

Olivia is forced to admire Lady Spencer's standards of conduct to the end, for when after Rollo's car accident his mother actually remembered to telephone to the despairing Olivia, the latter thought: "Oh, she's wonderful! . . . Lady Spencer, you've won. I'm beholden" (p. 347).

And yet it is impossible for Olivia—as it is for Lady Spencer's own daughter Marigold—to live the life that Lady Spencer and her own mother stand for. She cannot accept their assumptions, but her new independence, due to her changed position in society, leaves her life empty, for deep inside—like another rebel, Dinah in *The Echoing Grove*—Olivia longs for the permanence that her Bohemian style of life cannot give.

A chronologically earlier female rebel against social conventions in the fiction of Rosamond Lehmann is Mrs. Jardine in *The Ballad and the Source*. She would not accept a false role in her marriage and she took the first step to break away. She was full of high ideals about what the life of an independent modern woman should be like, and yet she fanatically clung to her life-long desperate attempt at justifying herself as a mother. She grew to see this role as the only one which could bring her a fulfilled life. It would be possible in her case only if she conformed to the social convention: this she could not do and society, as Mrs. Jardine saw it, took its revenge.

The fiction of Rosamond Lehmann covers the period from before the First World War (*The Ballad and the Source*) to the times shortly after the end of the Second War (*The Echoing Grove*). The picture it gives of the English middle and upper classes, the social tensions, and the general atmosphere of the fragmentation of life experienced by the younger generation, make the novels documents of their time that deserve to be placed in the mainstream of the English novelistic tradition.

Conclusion

A presentation of the subjective vision of life as the organizing principle of the novels of Rosamond Lehmann has been the aim of this thesis. A close connection between the subjective vision of life and the general cultural climate of the age has also been indicated. Now I would like to consider in more general terms Rosamond Lehmann's position as a novelist in the modern world.

The importance of the novelist's technique, which was my concern in the first two chapters, cannot be overestimated in a discussion of the books' distinctive character, for, as Mark Schorer says

technique is the means by which the writer's experience, which is his subject matter, compels him to attend to it; technique is the only means he has of discovering, exploring, developing his subject, of conveying its meaning, and, finally, of evaluating it.[1]

Rosamond Lehmann's own critical statements on the novel make it clear that her own position is similar:

when all is said and done, novels are made with words. With words we make the dredging net, the matter, the texture and the shape. And verbal accuracy is indivisible, I think, from accuracy of vision; and this precision is indivisible from insight.[2]

Her advice to young writers is that

they should bear in mind that the novel is a piece of work to be *written* ... There is no such thing as an excellent badly written novel. The novelist must care tremendously about words, about every word in every phrase, every sentence, every paragraph; about the rhythms of prose, which can be as subtle as those of poetry, and although less concentrated, should give almost if not quite as much trouble in the making. Above all, the novelist must listen accurately to what people say and to the way they say it. A live ear for dialogue is both rare and essential. Without it, the novel is as dead as mutton.[3]

A care and love for words and the novel's form manifests itself in all Rosamond Lehmann's books. She has been given credit as a writer of

---

[1] Mark Schorer, "Technique as Discovery", in *Forms of Modern Fiction,* ed. W. van O'Connor (Minneapolis: The Univ. of Minnesota Press, 1948), p. 9.
[2] "Rosamond Lehmann Reading", in John Lehmann, "New Soundings", *New World Writing,* II (1952), 49.
[3] Lehmann, "The Future of the Novel?", *Britain Today,* CXXII (June 1946), p. 9.

outstanding technical brilliance and sensitivity,[4] a consummate stylist,[5] and "a serious craftsman, and experimentalist in her art".[6] The accomplished quality of her prose has become, I believe, evident in the numerous quotations from her novels throughout this dissertation.

As we have seen, there exists a close relation between the conscious concern with the form of fiction and the modern writer's situation in a world in which the breakdown of values has brought about the necessity of searching for new patterns of meaning and artistic expression. N. A. Scott writes about Jane Austen that she was, like all older writers

> lucky because, in receiving her ultimate terms of reference from her culture, she was relieved of any uncertainty about how to establish contact with her readers and was, therefore, enabled to make the kinds of assumptions that facilitate the poetic transaction.[7]

The modern writer, however, has to find his own voice in order to express his personal vision of life. Often he has to construct his own frame of reference:

> Inheriting no traditional and widely accepted frame of values from his culture, before his art could be steadied by some executive principle of valuation, it has been necessary for the artist to try to construct some viable system of belief for himself, by means of an effort of personal vision. He has had to be, in a sense, his own priest, his own guide, his own Virgil. He has been condemned by the cultural circumstances of his time to draw from within himself everything that forms and orders his art . . . he has had to plunge deep in his search for the principles by which the anarchy of experience might be controlled and given a shape and a significance.[8]

Even if the artist does not succeed in the search for these "ordering principles", an awareness of this special situation is one of the distinctive marks of the modern writer as defined by Stephen Spender. In his book *The Struggle of the Modern* (1963), he contrasts the modern with the merely contemporary. The contemporary, while often critical of the modern world, accepts its basic values of rationality and progress (Spender's examples are Wells and Shaw), and usually takes sides in the contemporary social conflicts; in his work he uses a realist prose method. The moderns, on the other hand, use a poetic method in fiction, because such a method is better suited to conveying their preoccupation with "the real nature of the consciousness of the individual of acute sensibility in the modern world".[9]

---

[4] S. J. Kunitz, ed. *Twentieth Century Authors: A Biographical Dictionary of Modern Literature* (New York: The W. H. Wilson Company, 1955).

[5] LeStourgeon, p. 8.

[6] Victoria Sackville-West, "The Eternal Game", *The Spectator,* CXC (April 10, 1953), p. 454.

[7] Nathan A. Scott, Jr., "The Broken Center: A Definition of the Crisis of Values in Modern Literature", in *Symbolism in Religion and Literature,* ed. Rollo May (New York: G. Braziller, 1960), p. 185.

[8] Ibid.

[9] Stephen Spender, *The Struggle of the Modern* (London: Methuen, 1965), p. 130.

The contemporary method is "sociological", while the modern one is "seismographic", essentially imagistic.[10]

Rosamond Lehmann's conception of the novel is definitely modern in Spender's sense. She believes that

There is a "still centre" for the novelist as for any other artist. He or she who has not discovered it, or refuses the patience and concentration necessary to remain within it, will never produce a work of art, however brilliant and fertile his or her ideas for plot and characterization. Authors who have a perfectly clear scheme laid out for their novels, and can "tell you the plot" in detail from the outset may (or may not) produce a lively piece of entertainment or a stark chunk of social realism, but they have nothing to do with the novel as a work of art. For this kind, the same is true as for poetry: its genesis is the image, or isolated images which have become embedded in the mass of accumulated material in the author's "centre". When the moment comes (it cannot be predicted, but can be helped by the right kind of passivity) these images will start to become pregnant, to illuminate one another, to condense and form hitherto unsuspected relationships.[11]

The role of an image is central to the novel's inception:

Virginia Woolf once told me that the genesis of *The Waves* was a kind of vision of "a fin turning in a waste of waters" ... and that the rhythms of her diction, so striking and indeed uncharacteristic of her in its steady processional beat, arose out of watching moths coming in and out of the darkness toward a lighted lamp while she sat on her verandah.[12]

In the same article Rosamond Lehmann mentions (as far as I know it is the only critical comment on her own writing) the origins of *The Ballad and the Source*:

[It] sprang ... from childhood memories of a round green hill with a church at the top and a garden wall with a small door in it; of a portion of a little French river choked with water-lilies, with a weir in it and an inn on its banks, which for some inexplicable reason impressed itself upon my imagination years ago as the place where something that I would one day cause to happen, would happen; and from the image ... of a woman's figure in a blue cloak. But in offering these clues, let me not be misunderstood as implying a claim to have succeeded in my object. That object?—the object of every seriously undertaken novel: "the non-poetic statement of a poetic truth".[13]

Another central concept in Rosamond Lehmann's discussion of the novel is the character. Discussing the situation of the modern novel in 1946, she maintains that the reason for the present lack of great novels is

a dismal absence of people to fall in love with. Until the novel gives them back to us, commits itself and them whole-heartedly again, as in the old days, the novel will be small and cold, however sharp and bright ...

---

[10] Cf. ibid., p. 117.
[11] "The Future of the Novel?", p. 9.
[12] Ibid., p. 10.
[13] Ibid.

Novelists must be able to love men and women. Their greatness depends on this. Appreciation, compassion for humanity is what the great nineteenth century novelists felt ... They criticized human beings, they laughed at them, they condemned their wicked ways, but they loved and believed in them enough to endow their heroes and heroines with a moral stature which time cannot affect. This is why during the stress and horror of war sensitive people turned back to the past for their novels ... It was because they wanted to be with people whom they could love and admire, rather than with the impoverished, so frequently non-adult, dull and neurotic novel-figure of to-day.[14]

Looking at the development of the novel in the past decades it may seem that such an attitude is slightly old-fashioned. As long ago as the twenties Ortega y Gasset, in his *Notes on the Novel*, commented on the "dehumanization of art", and in our own day writers like Robbe-Grillet assume that the novel of character is definitely dead:

In fact, the creators of character, in the traditional sense, can now do nothing more than present us with puppets in whom they themselves no longer believe. The novel that contains characters belongs well and truly to the past, it was peculiar to an age—that of the apogee of the individual.[15]

And yet, at least in England, Rosamond Lehmann's belief in the supremacy of character is still going strong. It is shared by such important critics as John Bayley (*The Characters of Love*, 1960), Iris Murdoch ("Against Dryness", 1961), and W. J. Harvey (*Character and the Novel,* 1965). Bernard Bergonzi, in his excellent *The Situation of the Novel* (1970), agrees with these critics that "a humanistic view of literature should enjoin both writer and reader to respect and even love the characters of a novel."[16] He is aware, nevertheless, that this attitude

is historically conditioned, and that its end may be in sight for ... the liberal and individualistic virtues so marvellously preserved and crystallized in the traditional novel are, indeed, on the retreat over a large part of the globe, and have been continuously on the defensive ever since 1914.[17]

Rosamond Lehmann encounters the modern dilemma as a creator of characters who is conscious of the present lack of a common frame of reference. How then is a novelist to create a convincing and "lovable" character? E. M. Forster wrote that a character in a novel is real

when the novelist knows everything about it. He may not choose to tell us all he knows—many of the facts, even of the kind we call obvious, may be hidden. But he will give us the feeling that though the character has not been explained, it is explicable, and we get from this a reality of a kind we can never get in daily life.[18]

[14] Ibid., pp. 9—10.
[15] Alain Robbe-Grillet, *Towards a New Novel*. Quoted after Bernard Bergonzi, *The Situation of the Novel* (Harmondsworth: Penguin, 1972), p. 45.
[16] Bergonzi, p. 61.
[17] Ibid., pp. 61—62.
[18] Forster, p. 63.

Rosamond Lehmann's solution seems to be a limitation of her range of characters to those she "knows everything about". It is characteristic that she chooses to present almost exclusively the experience of young girls and women. She writes about an essentially feminine world and the "femininity" of her art is of such an order that, in the words of a fellow novelist, William Plomer, "one can think of no higher praise".[19] It is just because Rosamond Lehmann does not venture beyond what she knows perfectly well, that it is possible to say about *The Weather in the Streets*: "As a picture of certain aspects of contemporary life it could scarcely be better, for Miss Lehmann knows, as they say, her stuff, and knows it through and through. She is just as strong on family life as on the circumstances surrounding adultery and abortion ..."[20] Portraying, as she does, familiar scenes and experiences, Rosamond Lehmann comes time and again to the same types of people in her novels. Judith (*Dusty Answer*), Rebecca (*The Ballad and the Source*) and Olivia (*Invitation to the Waltz*) have very much in common, just as is the case with Olivia (*The Weather in the Streets*) and Dinah (*The Echoing Grove*) —two "black sheep" of the family. Mrs. Curtis, Lady Spencer, and Mrs. Burkett, all mothers of a family nursing their husbands, are strong characters living by the traditional clear-cut values, no longer acceptable to their more rebellious daughters. Kate and Madeleine are the conventional daughters, Mary Seddon and Mrs. Jardine the women with a past, Charlie and Guy the charming and promising young men who died in the war.

Rosamond Lehmann's novels are not distinguished by new topics or exploration of concealed motives, but by a highly individual and on the whole successful treatment of familiar subject matter. This poses the question of the critical assessment of a novelist's achievement in terms of the range of his work. Graham Hough's discussion of this problem is relevant here. Speaking about the nature of the novel in general, he observes that

it characteristically purports to represent the state of society at a particular time in a particular place; and part of its merit seems to be that it does it justly ... there is a sense in which all novels are historical novels. At any rate the novel has an undefined frontier with history, and part of its characteristic merit is historical—a report on social reality.[21]

It does not matter, however, whether a novel offers a panoramic view of society or whether it presents just a small section of it. Hough's defence of a socially restricted novel seems to be particularly apt and, since Rosamond Lehmann does indeed describe a very limited segment of society—which in itself quite wrongly becomes today a cause for censure—I would like to quote his argument in full:

[19] William Plomer, "Fiction", *The Spectator*, CLVII (July 17, 1936), p. 110.
[20] Ibid.
[21] Graham Hough, *An Essay in Criticism* (London: Duckworth, 1956), pp. 56—57.

We should be wrong ... to judge a novel by the *amount* of social and historical reality that it incorporates. It is not a qualitative matter. The novelist is perfectly apt to make his own selection from the available social and historical material, and it may be a narrow one. We do not ask in reading Jane Austen "But where are the lower classes?" Or if we do we are foolish. Jane Austen tells the truth about a certain segment of the middle class of her time, from the viewpoint of a woman who herself belongs to that class. And it is enough. If we want we can deduce a great deal from the presented material about social areas of which she tells us little or nothing. If we want to see how much more could have been put in we can turn to George Eliot; but George Eliot is not to be preferred on that account.[22]

A. A. Mendilow says that "fiction as a representational or thematic art responds very sensitively to the pressures of the age; the lesser mirrors, the greater interprets to people their modes of behaviour and thought."[23] Rosamond Lehmann's novels of the subjective vision of life are such a response to the "pressures of the age". If they are not great novels, they are certainly what Robert Liddell calls good novels of the type "minor classics".[24] This is as far as I would venture to go in "giving marks" to a novelist. The ultimate question is whether a novel "is or is not a work of creative imagination"[25]—and in my opinion the novels of Rosamond Lehmann pass this test.

[22] Ibid., p. 114.
[23] Mendilow, p. 30.
[24] Robert Liddell, *A Treatise on the Novel* (London: Cape, J., 1955), p. 20.
[25] Charles Morgan, "Creative Imagination", in *English Critical Essays: Twentieth Century*. Selected by Derek Hudson (London: Oxford Univ. Press, 1960), p. 66.

Selected Bibliography

Primary Sources

(Works by Rosamond Lehmann)

1. Novels (first editions)
   The Ballad and the Source. London, Collins, 1944.
   Dusty Answer. London: Chatto, 1927.
   The Echoing Grove. London: Collins, 1953.
   Invitation to the Waltz. London: Chatto, 1932.
   A Note in Music. London: Chatto, 1930.
   The Weather in the Streets. London: Collins, 1936.

2. Short stories
   The Gipsy's Baby and Other Stories. London: Collins, 1946.

3. Play
   No More Music. London: Collins, 1939.

4. Miscellaneous (for a complete listing of Rosamond Lehmann's poems and the translations of her works see Margaret T. Gustafson, "Rosamond Lehmann: A Bibliography", in *Twentieth Century Literature: A Scholarly and Critical Journal* Vol. IV, 58—59.)
   "Books in General". *New Statesman and Nation,* 29 (March 3, 1945), 143.

   Cassou, Jean. "Letter to Cousin Mary". Trans. R. Lehmann. *New Writing, 2.* London: Bodley Head, 1936.

   Cocteau, Jean. *Children of the Game.* Trans. R. Lehmann. London: Harvill, 1955.

   "Dylan Thomas". *Spectator,* 191 (Nov. 20, 1953), 574.

   "For Virginia Woolf". *The Penguin New Writing.* VII (June, 1941), 53—58.

   "The Future of the Novel?" *Britain Today.* No. CXII (June, 1946), 5—11.

   Lemarchand, Jacques. *Geneviève.* Trans. R. Lehmann. London: Lehmann, 1947.

   "Letter to a Friend". *The Penguin New Writing.* V (April, 1941), 80—87.

   A Letter to a Sister. London: The Hogarth Press, 1931.

   Letters from our Daughters. R. Lehmann and Cynthia Lady Sandys. London: The College of Psychic Science, [1972].

   A Man Seen Afar. Wellesley Tudor Pole and R. Lehmann. London: Neville Spearman, 1965.

   "Miss Rosamond Lehmann". *New Statesman and Nation* 47 (Jan. 30, 1954), 131.

"Mr. Coward's Play". *Spectator.* 167 (July 18, 1941), 61.

"Rosamond Lehmann Reading". In John Lehmann, "New Soundings". *New World Writing.* II (1952), 41—57.

The Swan in the Evening: Fragments of an Inner Life. London: Collins, 1967.

Secondary sources
(Criticism of Rosamond Lehmann — List of Works consulted)

Allen, Walter. *Tradition and Dream.* London: Phoenix House, 1964, pp. 195—97.

Bentley, Phyllis. "A Satire and Some Stories", *The New Statesman and Nation.* N.S. IV (October 15, 1932), 454.

Bowen, Elizabeth. "The Modern Novel and the Theme of Love", *New Republic.* CXXVIII (May 11, 1953), 18—19.

Burgess, Anthony. *The Novel Now: A Student's Guide to Contemporary Fiction.* London: Faber & Faber, 1971, pp. 123—24.

Cahuet, Alberic. "Rosamond Lehmann et les romancieres britanniques", *L'Illustration.* CLXXXVI (September 16, 1933), 90—91.

Chamberlain, John. "Miss Lehmann's Second Novel, *A Note in Music",* New York *Herald Tribune Books.* October 30, 1932, p. 6.

Dangerfield, George. "Rosamond Lehmann and the Perilous Enchantment of Things Past", *The Bookman,* LXXVI (February, 1933), 172—76.

Haxton Britten, Florence. "The Gospel of Resignation", *New York Harald Tribune Books.* September 7, 1930, p. 4.

Karl, Frederick R. *A Reader's Guide to the Contemporary English Novel.* London: Thames & Hudson, 1972, p. 279.

Krutch, Joseph Wood. "All for Love", *The Nation.* CXLII (June 3, 1936), 713—14.

Kunitz, Stanley J., ed. *Twentieth Century Authors: A Biographical Dictionary of Modern Literature.* First Supplement. New York: The H. W. Wilson Company, 1955.

Lehmann, John. *The Ample Propositon.* London: Eyre and Spottiswoode, 1966.

— *I Am My Brother.* London: Longmans, 1960.

— *The Whispering Gallery.* London: Longmans, 1955.

LeStourgeon, Diana E. *Rosamond Lehmann.* New York: Twayne Publishers, Inc., 1965.

Longaker, Mark and Edwin C. Bolles. *Contemporary English Literature.* New York: Appleton, 1953.

Loveman, Amy. "What Every Woman Knows", *Saturday Review of Literature,* Vol. 9 (1932—33), 219.

Marković, Vida E. *The Changing Face: Disintegration of Personality in the Twentieth-Century British Novel, 1900—1950.* Carbondale: Southern Illinois Univ. Press, 1970, pp. 97—111.

McCormick, John. *Catastrophe and Imagination: An Interpretation of the Recent English and American Novel.* London: Longmans, 1957, pp. 75, 85—86, 89—92, 159, 165, 229.

Mortimer, Raymond. "Two Novels", *The New Statesman and Nation.* N.S. XXVIII (December 30, 1944), 224.

"On an Author", *New York Herald Tribune Book Review.* June 14, 1953, p. 2.

"One of the James Girls", Newsweek. XXV (April 9, 1945), 93—94.

Paterson, Isabel. "April Moods of Girlhood", *New York Herald Tribune Books.* October 30, 1932, p. 5.

Patterson, Isabel. "One Woman Who Missed Her Way in Love: Rosamond Lehmann's Delicate Analysis of Illusion and Reality", *New York Herald Tribune Books*. May 17, 1936, p. 1.

Peterson, Virgilia. "Those Experiences of the Heart", *New York Herald Tribune Books*. May 10, 1953, pp. 1, 8.

Plomer, William. "Fiction", *The Spectator*. CLVII (July 17, 1936), 110.

Proteus. "New Novels", *The New Statesman*. XXXV (August 23, 1930), 622–23.

Sackville-West, Victoria. "The Eternal Game", *The Spectator*. CXC (April 10, 1953), 454.

Scott-James, R. A. *Fifty Years of English Literature: 1900–1950*. London: Longmans, 1951, pp. 180–182.

Shuman, R. Baird. "Personal Isolation in the Novels of Rosamond Lehmann," *Revue des Langues Vivantes*. XXVI (January, 1960), pp. 76–80.

Spender, Stephen. *World Within World*. London: Hamish Hamilton, 1951, p. 143.

Tracy, Honor. "New Novels", *The New Statesman and Nation*. N.S. XLV (April 11, 1953), 433–34.

Trilling, Diana. "Fiction in Review", *The Nation*. CLX (April 14, 1945), 422–23.

Warner, Oliver, "Rosamond Lehmann", *The Bookman*. LXXXVII (December, 1934), 174.

Woolf, Leonard. "The World of Books: Rhapsody or Dusty Answer?" *The Nation & Athenaeum*. XLI (September 10, 1927), 749.

Other Works

(Only works referred to in the text are included)

Auerbach, Erich. *Mimesis: The Representation of Reality in Western Literature*. Trans. Willard R. Trask. Princeton: Princeton Univ. Press, 1968.

Austen, Jane. *Pride and Prejudice*. London: Bentley, 1891.

Austen, Jane. *Sense and Sensibility*. Harmondsworth: Penguin, 1971.

Bayley, John. *The Characters of Love: A Study in the Literature of Personality*. London: Constable, 1960.

Beach, Joseph Warren. *The Twentieth Century Novel: Studies in Technique*. New York: Appleton, 1932.

Bell, Quentin. *Virginia Woolf: A Biography. Vol. 1: 1882–1912, Vol. 2: 1912–1941*. London: The Hogarth Press, 1972.

Bergonzi, Bernard. *The Situation of the Novel*. Harmondsworth: Pelican, 1972.

Björck, Staffan. *Romanens formvärld: Studier i prosaberättarens teknik*. Stockholm: Natur och Kultur, 1968.

Blake, William. *Poems and Prophesies*. London, New York: Everyman's Library, 1970.

Booth, Wayne C. *The Rhetoric of Fiction*. Chicago: Univ. of Chicago Press, 1961.

Bradbury, Malcolm. *Possibilities: Essays on the State of the Novel*. London, Oxford, New York: Oxford Univ. Press, 1973.

Brown, E. K. *Rhythm in the Novel*. Toronto: University of Toronto Press, 1950.

Burgess, Anthony. *The Novel Now: A Student's Guide to Contemporary Fiction*. London: Faber & Faber, 1971.

Crews, Frederick C. *E. M. Forster: The Perils of Humanism*. Princeton: Princeton Univ. Press, 1962.

Daiches, David. *The Novel and the Modern World*. Chicago: Chicago Univ. Press, 1948.

— *A Study of Literature.* New York: Cornell Univ. Press, 1948.

Dictionary of World Literary Terms. Ed. J. T. Shipley. London: Allen & Unwin, 1970.

Edel, Leon. *The Psychological Novel: 1900—1950.* New York: J. B. Lippincott Co., 1955.

Epstein, E. L. "The Irrelevant Narrator: A Stylistic Note on the Place of the Author in Contemporary Technique of the Novel". *Language and Style.* Winter 1969. Southern Illinois Univ., p. 93.

O'Faolain, Sean. *The Vanishing Hero: Studies in Novelists of the Twenties.* New York: Books for Libraries Press, 1956.

Fordham, Frieda. *An Introduction to Jung's Psychology.* Harmondsworth: Penguin, 1964.

Forster, E. M. *Aspects of the Novel.* New York: Harcourt, 1954.

Freedman, Ralph. *The Lyrical Novel.* Princeton: Princeton Univ. Press, 1963.

Friedman, Alan. *The Turn of the Novel: The Transition to Modern Fiction.* London, Oxford, New York: Oxford Univ. Press, 1966.

Van Ghent, Dorothy. *The English Novel: Form and Function.* New York: Reinhart, 1953.

Gordon, Robert C. *Under Which King? A Study of the Scottish Waverley Novels.* Edinburgh, London: Oliver & Boyd, 1969.

Harvey, W. J. *Character and the Novel.* London: Chatto, 1965.

Hatcher, Anna G. "Voir as a Modern Novelistic Device", *Philological Quarterly.* XXIII (1944), 354—74.

Hayden, John O., ed. *Scott: The Critical Heritage.* London: Routledge, 1970.

Hough, Graham. *An Essay on Criticism.* London: Duckworth, 1966.

Isaacs, J. *An Assessment of Twentieth-Century Literature.* London: Secker & Warburg, 1951.

James, Henry. "Anthony Trollope". *Theory of Fiction: Henry James.* Ed. J. E. Miller, Jr. Lincoln: Univ. of Nebraska, 1972.

— "The Art of Fiction". *Selected Literary Criticism.* Ed. M. Shapira. Harmondsworth: Penguin, 1963.

— *The Art of the Novel: Critical Prefaces.* Ed. R. P. Blackmur. New York, London: Scribner, 1935.

— *What Maisie Knew.* London: Oxford Univ. Press, 1966.

Langer, Susanne. *Feeling and Form: A Theory of Art.* New York: Scribner, 1953.

Liddell, Robert. *A Treatise on the Novel.* London: Cape, J., 1955.

May, Rollo. *Love and Will.* London: Collins, 1972.

Mendilow, A. A. *Time and the Novel.* New York: Humanities Press, 1972.

Morgan, Charles. "Creative Imagination", in *English Critical Essays: Twentieth Century.* Selected by Derek Hudson. London: Oxford University Press, 1968.

Murdoch, Iris. "Against Dryness", *Encounter* 1961.

Myers, Walter L. *The Later Realism: A Study of Characterization in the British Novel.* Chicago: Chicago Univ. Press, 1927.

Ortega y Gasset, José. *The Dehumanization of Art and Other Essays on Art, Culture and Literature.* Princeton: Princeton Univ. Press, 1948.

Pearson, Hesketh. *Walter Scott: His Life and Personality.* London: Methuen, 1954.

Raban, Jonathan. *The Techniques of Modern Fiction: Essays in Practical Criticism.* London: Notre Dame Univ. Press, 1969.

Routh, H. V. *English Literature and Ideas in the Twentieth Century.* London: Methuen, 1946.

Schorer, Mark. *The Novelist in the Modern World.* Tucson: Univ. of Arizona, 1957.

— *Society and Self in the Novel.* New York: Columbia University Press, 1956.

— "Technique as Discovery", in *Forms of Modern Fiction: Essays collected in Honor*

139

of Joseph Warren Beach. Ed. W. van O'Connor. Minneapolis: The Univ. of Minnesota Press, 1948.

Scott, Nathan A. Jr. "The Broken Center: A Definition of the Crisis of Values in Modern Literature", in *Symbolism in Religion and Literature*. Ed. Rollo May. New York: G. Braziller, 1960.

Scott, Walter. *The Journal*. 2 Vols. New York: Harper & Brothers, 1891.

— *Quentin Durward*. New York: Airmont Publishing Co., 1967.

Spender, Stephen. *The Struggle of the Modern*. London: Methuen, 1965.

Tate, Allen. "Techniques of Fiction", *Sewanee Review*. LII (1944), 210—25.

Trilling, Lionel. "Art and Fortune", in *The Liberal Imagination*. New York: Doubleday, 1957.

Wellek, René. *Concepts of Criticism*. New Haven, London: Yale Univ. Press, 1963.

Wellek, René and Austin Warren. *Theory of Literature*. Harmondsworth: Penguin, 1963.

West, Paul. *The Modern Novel*. London: Hutchinson, 1963.

Wilson, Edmund. *Axel's Castle: A Study in the Imaginative Literature of 1870—1930*. New York: Scribner, 1955.

Wimsatt, W. K. Jr. and Cleanth Brooks. *Literary Criticism: A Short History*. New York: Routledge, 1957.

Woolf, Virginia. "How It Strikes a Contemporary", *The Common Reader*. London: The Hogarth Press, 1940.

— "Modern Fiction", *The Common Reader*. London: The Hogarth Press, 1948.

— "Mr. Bennett and Mrs. Brown", *The Captain's Death Bed*. London: The Hogarth Press, 1950.

— *Mrs. Dalloway*. Harmondsworth: Penguin, 1972.

— *Night and Day*. London: The Hogarth Press, 1960.